Essential Histories

The Indian Mutiny 1857–58

Essential Histories

The Indian Mutiny 1857–58

Gregory Fremont-Barnes

First published in Great Britain in 2007 by Osprey Publishing,
Midland House, West Way, Botley, Oxford OX2 0PH, UK
443 Park Avenue South, New York, NY 10016, USA
E-mail: info@ospreypublishing.com

A CIP catalogue record for this book is available from the
British Library

ISBN: 978 1 84603 209 7

Page layout by: Ken Vail Graphic Design, Cambridge, UK
Index by Alan Thatcher
Typeset in GillSans and I Stone seriff
Maps by The Map Studio
Originated by United Graphic Pte Ltd, Singapore
Printed in China through Bookbuilders

07 08 09 10 11   10 9 8 7 6 5 4 3 2 1

For a catalogue of all books published by Osprey Military and
Aviation please contact:

NORTH AMERICA
Osprey Direct, c/o Random House Distribution Center,
400 Hahn Road, Westminster, MD 21157
E-mail: info@ospreydirect.com

ALL OTHER REGIONS
Osprey Direct UK, P.O. Box 140 Wellingborough, Northants,
NN8 2FA, UK
E-mail: info@ospreydirect.co.uk

www.ospreypublishing.com

Author's note
Conflicting attempts at the transliteration of names from Hindi
and other Indian languages have resulted in various alternative
forms of spelling for persons and places, for instance:
Tantya Tope/Tantia Topi; Oude/Oudh; Kanpur/Cawnpore;
Amballa/Umballa; Barrackpur/Barrackpore; Mungul Pandy/
Mangal Pandy/ Mungal Pandy; Moghul/Mughal; Brahman/Brahmin;
Dum Dum/Dum-Dum; Mirath/Meerut; Bibighur/Bibighar. Where
variations occur, the most common form used at the time of the
Mutiny has been employed.

Contents

Introduction

In August 1855, the newly appointed Governor-General of India, Lord Canning, made a remark during a speech in London which was to prove remarkably prophetic. 'We must not forget,' he said,

> that in the sky of India, serene as it is, a cloud may arise, at first no bigger than a man's hand, but which growing bigger and bigger, may at last threaten to overwhelm us with ruin. What has happened once may happen again. The disturbing causes have diminished certainly, but they are not dispelled.

Canning could not have known when he made this oblique reference that mutiny was not only imminent, but destined to explode into a full-scale conflict of exceptional brutality.

Following the end of the Napoleonic Wars in 1815, the British Army fought in numerous minor colonial conflicts, but did not confront another European army until the Crimean War (1854–56) when, notwithstanding Britain's ultimate success, the war revealed numerous problems, above all a shockingly poor system of supply and transport: the army was unaccustomed to conducting large-scale operations. No sooner were military authorities implementing reforms to reap some benefit from the lessons learned in the Crimea than British troops faced a far greater challenge: the Indian Mutiny.

The story of the Mutiny is rife with drama: the opening days of incendiarism and indiscriminate murder; the treacherous massacre of women and children at

Storming of the Kashmir Gate, Delhi. Once inside the city, British troops, bent on revenge for the massacre of their compatriots at Cawnpore and elsewhere, went on an orgy of plunder and murder. (National Army Museum)

Captain Dighton Probyn, 2nd Punjab Cavalry, in action at Agra, 10 October 1857. Probyn's regiment was but one of a number of mounted Sikh irregular units.

Cawnpore; the heroism of the Lucknow garrison which, besieged in the ruins of the British Residency for three months, defiantly held out amidst the most appalling conditions and lost two-thirds of its number; the fearful retribution exacted by British authorities in response to the murder of their civilians; the mismatched forces at the siege of Delhi; and the ferocity which characterized fighting in which quarter was neither asked nor granted.

It is essential, from the outset, to lay down some parameters and debunk some of the more familiar myths associated with this subject. The very name 'Indian Mutiny' has been challenged, especially by some Indian scholars, as an inaccurate description of the conflict which raged across northern and central India in 1857–58. To many on the sub-continent it is better known as 'The First War of Independence' – a war of national liberation. To contemporary Britons, it was variously known as 'The Great Rebellion', 'The Sepoy Revolt', or 'The Great Mutiny'. Whatever name one ascribes to the event, there is no foundation to the claim that the Mutiny was a national rebellion much less a war of independence, for the revolt affected only a portion of Indian forces in British service, the remainder of whom remained loyal to the Raj. Moreover, many Indian rulers and states declined to join the revolt, or indeed lent their active support to the British in their suppression of it. It is not insignificant that nearly half of the many thousands who took refuge in the Residency at Lucknow were sepoys (Indian troops) loyal to the Crown and Indian civilians seeking British protection. In short, without the substantial contribution made by loyal Indians, Britain might very well have lost its most important colonial possession.

The Mutiny must, therefore, above all else, not be characterized as a straightforward conflict between Briton and Indian, for large numbers of Indians across the sub-continent played a key role in the re-establishment of British imperial authority in India.

Yet the limited nature of the revolt – largely confined to the East India Company's forces in Bengal – ought in no measure to minimize the threat it posed, nor the fact that the Mutiny was entirely confined to Indian troops, for support also came from various princes and rulers who sought the restoration of those hereditary rights or other privileges recently denied them by the East India Company, which administered

Lieutenant John Watson, 1st Punjab Cavalry, winning the Victoria Cross at Lucknow, 14 November 1857. (National Army Museum)

the sub-continent as an agent of the British government. Though the revolt did not constitute a fully fledged bid to throw off the colonial yoke and replace it with a nation-state in the sense that we would recognize today – no concerted thought was given to what form of government would replace the colonial administration – the Mutiny nevertheless had a serious political dimension to it.

As for the causes of the conflict, their roots lay rather deeper than the sepoys' refusal to use the greased cartridges for the new Enfield rifle: it was a major conflict in its own right, fundamentally a struggle between rival cultural and religious perspectives, principally based on the perception of some Indians – mostly Hindus but some Muslims as well – that British rule threatened their respective faiths. For many Britons, the Mutiny – fought in the midst of a period of Christian revival at home – represented a moral struggle of good versus evil, Christian against heathen, and civilization against barbarism. Missionary zeal and the eagerness for converts not only yielded meagre results: it sparked the most viciously fought conflict in British imperial history.

India in 1857

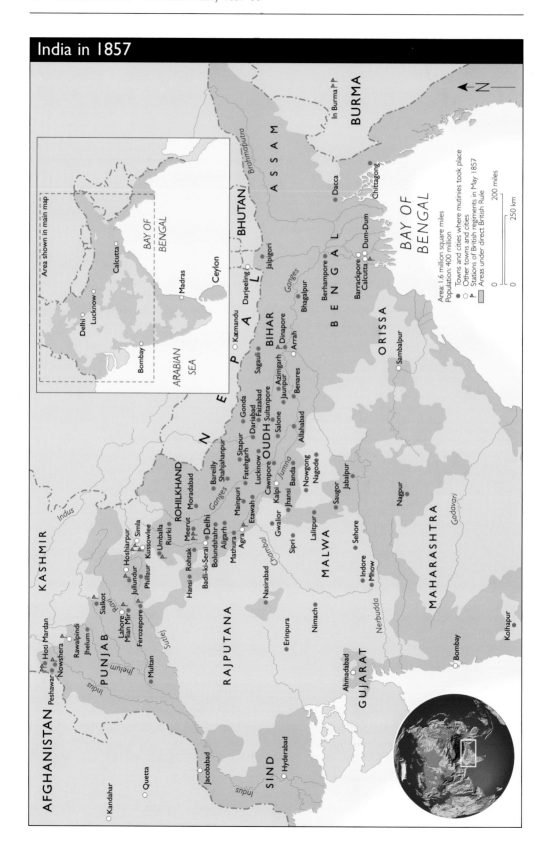

Area: 1.6 million square miles
Population: 400 million

● Towns and cities where mutinies took place
○ Other towns and cities
▲ Stations of British regiments in May 1857
░ Areas under direct British Rule

0 — 200 miles
0 — 250 km

Chronology

1857 January Rumour begins at the Dum-Dum musketry depot, near Calcutta, that British military authorities have deliberately greased the new Enfield rifle cartridges with the fat of pigs and cows

26 February Sepoys of the 19th Native Infantry at Berhampore in Bengal refuse rifle practice, notwithstanding their being issued with ungreased cartridges

29 March At Barrackpore, in Bengal, Mungal Pandy, a sepoy of the 34th Native Infantry, wounds two British officers during an unsuccessful attempt to incite his unit to mutiny

31 March 19th Native Infantry disbanded at Barrackpore for the mutinous behaviour of 26 February

8 April Mungal Pandy hanged at Barrackpore

24 April Eighty-five troopers of the 3rd Bengal Light Cavalry at Meerut refuse orders to fire greased cartridges

6 May Part of the 34th Native Infantry disbanded at Barrackpore for their disobedience on 29 March

8 May Troops of the 3rd Bengal Light Cavalry found guilty by court-martial and given severe sentences

9 May In Meerut, convicted prisoners chained in the presence of the entire command and imprisoned

10 May Native troops revolt at Meerut, massacre the British cantonment, and march on Delhi

11 May Mutineers arrive at Delhi from Meerut, combine forces with local garrison and murder Europeans and Indian Christians

13 May Bahadur Shah II proclaimed new Mughal emperor. British disarm the native garrison at Lahore, in the Punjab

17 May Delhi Field Force, under General George Anson, Commander-in-Chief of India, advances from Umballa

20–23 May Part of the 9th Native Infantry mutinies near Agra

27 May Anson dies of cholera; replaced by Major-General Sir Henry Barnard

30 May Garrison at Lucknow mutinies; mutineers there dispersed or disarmed

31 May Mutinies in Rohilkhand

May–July Brigadier-General John Nicholson's 'Moveable Column' disarms regiments in the Punjab

3–14 June Mutinies and massacres at posts across Oudh, the North-West Provinces, central India, Rajputana and the Punjab

6 June Major-General Sir Hugh Wheeler besieged at Cawnpore by native garrison

8 June Major-General Sir Henry Barnard, in command of the Delhi Field Force plus the garrison at Meerut, defeats the rebels at Badli-ki-Serai and establishes himself on the Ridge north of Delhi

27 June British garrison massacred at Cawnpore after Nana Sahib treacherously violates an agreement to allow safe passage down the Ganges; surviving women and children imprisoned

30 June Rebels defeat Sir Henry Lawrence, commander at Lucknow, at Chinhut; siege of Residency begins

5 July General Barnard dies of cholera; Major-General Thomas Reed succeeds as commander of the Delhi Field Force

12 July Brigadier-General Sir Henry Havelock defeats rebels at Fatehpur, en route to Cawnpore

15 July Havelock defeats rebels at Aong and Pandu Nadi, near Cawnpore. His approach prompts Nana Sahib to order massacre of women and children captives at Cawnpore

16 July Havelock defeats rebel force under Nana Sahib's personal command near Cawnpore

17 July Havelock enters Cawnpore and discovers evidence of the massacre. Sir Archdale Wilson replaces the ailing Reed as commander of the Delhi Field Force

31 July Lord Canning, Governor-General of India, issues his controversial 'Clemency' resolution, by which he advises against the execution of mutineers not convicted of murder

13 August General Sir Colin Campbell, Anson's successor as Commander-in-Chief of India, arrives at Calcutta

14 August Nicholson's 'Moveable Column' arrives at the British camp in front of Delhi

17 August Major William Hobson defeats a large body of rebel cavalry near Rohtak

4 September Siege train, proceeding from the Punjab, arrives in the British camp outside Delhi

14 September Wilson begins assault on Delhi

19 September Havelock and Sir James Outram advance on Lucknow

20 September Delhi completely cleared of mutineers

23 September Nicholson, mortally wounded by a musket shot during the assault of the 14th, dies

25 September First relief of the Residency at Lucknow by Havelock and Outram; garrison is enlarged, but remains under siege; Brigadier James Neill killed by a musket ball during the final advance

14–17 November Second relief of the Residency at Lucknow by Campbell

19–27 November Evacuation of Lucknow; garrison left at the Alambagh; Campbell marches on Cawnpore, which the rebels have re-occupied after Havelock's departure

24 November Havelock dies of dysentery at Lucknow in the midst of the evacuation

26–27 November Tantia Topi and the Gwalior Contingent defeat Major-General Windham in second battle of Cawnpore

28–30 November Campbell reaches Cawnpore to join Windham

6 December Campbell defeats Tantia Topi in the third battle of Cawnpore

1858   16 January Major-General Sir Hugh Rose begins campaign in central India

February Campbell opens separate campaign for reconquest of Oudh

3 February Rose relieves Saugor after a seven-month siege

2 March Campbell commences operations against Lucknow

11–21 March Assault and capture of Lucknow; rebels escape westwards

22 March Rose invests fortified city of Jhansi

April Campbell begins pacification of Oudh and Rohilkhand

1 April Dividing his force, Rose defeats a numerically superior rebel army under Tantia Topi on the river Betwa

3 April Rose captures Jhansi but the Rani of Jhansi escapes to Kalpi

15 April Major-General Walpole's column disastrously repulsed in an attack on the fort at Ruiya

5 May Campbell defeats rebel force at Bareilly

7 May Rose defeats large rebel force under Tantia Topi and the Rani of Jhansi at Kunch

22 May Rose defeats rebels at Kalpi; end of operations in Rohilkhand; start of guerrilla warfare

28 May The last substantial rebel force, under Rao Sahib, Tantia Topi, the Rani of Jhansi and the Nawab of

Banda enter the state of Gwalior with the remnants of their force and seize the city of the same name on 1 June

12 June Major-General Hope Grant defeats rebels at Nawabganj in the final decisive battle in Oudh

17 June Rani of Jhansi killed in action at Kotah-ki-Serai, near Gwalior

19 June Rose defeats the rebels at Gwalior and retakes the city; Tantia Topi flees

2 August Queen Victoria approves bill transferring administration of India from the East India Company to the Crown

1 November Queen's proclamation offers unconditional pardon to all rebels not involved in murder or the protection of murderers

1859 **4 January** Various Oudh rebel leaders, including Nana Sahib, forced into the Nepal *Terai* by Hope Grant

7 January Operations in Oudh declared officially over, though mopping-up operations continue

18 April Tantia Topi, captured on 7 April, after being betrayed to the British, is hanged

8 July Canning declares hostilities at an end throughout the sub-continent

Historical origins

Britain's connection with India began on 31 January 1600 when Queen Elizabeth I signed the charter of the East India Company, a major commercial enterprise which would compete with other European trading concerns for the spice trade on the sub-continent. They operated at the behest of the Mughal emperors, descendants of the Monguls of Genghiz Khan, who had occupied India in the 15th century. By the time the Company established trading posts, known as factories, on the coasts of India, Mughal rule was in a state of decline, with regular in-fighting between rival Indian princes. The power vacuum thus created enabled the Company to expand its power and influence, converting it from a purely business concern to an imperial agent of the Crown.

The East India Company's natural rival was its French counterpart, but when war broke out in Europe between Britain and France in the War of the Austrian Succession (1740–48), hostilities inevitably spread to India, where the Company maintained its own private forces which worked in conjunction with local native levies and regular British Army regiments. The French were eventually evicted from India during another mid-century conflict, the Seven Years' War (1756–63). Robert Clive, a clerk-turned-soldier in the East India Company, inflicted a decisive blow against the French and their Indian allies at the battle of Plassey in June 1757, which consolidated the Company's control over Bengal. From 1765 the Mughal emperor, in recognition of the Company's achievements, granted it the status of a feudatory ruler, and thereafter extended its hold over new territories through annexation, alliances and conquest.

In successive decades of the 18th century, Company forces defeated the sultans of southern India and took on the power of the Marathas of the north and west.

Robert Clive, victor of the battle of Plassey and one of his country's greatest military commanders. By conquering Bengal during the Seven Years' War he laid the foundation for British expansion across the sub-continent over the next century. (Philip Haythornthwaite)

By the early 19th century the Mughal dynasty had come to an ignominious end and the last emperor, based at his ancient capital of Delhi but wielding no effective power, had been reduced to a mere pensioner of the Company. It was a measure of British efficiency that by this time India, divided among the three 'presidencies' of Bengal, Madras and Bombay, could be managed by a small body of administrators backed by three different armies, themselves supported by regular troops of the British Army. Successive governors-general, appointed by the Crown and based at Calcutta, expanded the domains of British India over time, up to the administration of Lord Dalhousie, whose conquest of the Punjab over the course of two wars (1845–46, 1848–49) pushed the frontier against Afghanistan and broke independent Sikh power. By this time the Company had evolved from a commercial organization to an agency for the civil and military administration of much of the sub-continent.

The General Court Room, East India House. The East India Company's Court of Directors in London was accountable to the British government through the Board of Control, the president of which was appointed by the Prime Minister and occupied a seat in the cabinet. (British Library)

While the East India Company's rule brought benefits to Indian society, including peace, rule of law, an efficient civil service, political stability, improved roads and bridges, the introduction of the electric telegraph and the early stages of a railway system, its administration inevitably introduced unwelcome attitudes and institutions – some tolerated, some even admired – but others resented or even loathed. Specifically, the British applied laws and customs alien, and sometimes anathema to, Indian society, such as allowing widows to remarry, and the establishment of a land title system where none had previously existed, the result of which was the confiscation of land regarded by Indians as hereditary property.

Even within the regiments themselves, *esprit de corps* had undergone a gradual decline, first because the gradual expansion of Company forces with new regiments consisting of Gurkhas, Sikhs, Pathans and Punjabi Muslims gave rise to fears among Hindu troops of the Bengal Army that their importance and privileged position was on the decline, and secondly because relations between the younger generation of recently arrived British officers and the sepoys were not as close as in generations past.

Merchants, soldiers and administrators of the 18th century had often learned Indian languages, collected Indian art and artefacts, and even married Indian women. Some had adopted Indian lifestyles and practised Indian customs. While they never considered Indian culture superior to their own, they found much in it to admire.

By the Victorian era few men of this ilk still remained in India. With respect to Company officers in particular – beyond taking some pride in the leadership and proper management of their sepoys – few familiarized themselves with the languages, customs and beliefs of the Indian rank and file. Interest in, understanding of, and at times appreciation for, the religion, feelings and culture of their troops, gradually declined within the (entirely British) officer corps, with the erosion of mutual trust the inevitable by-product. In many cases, junior officers physically separated themselves from their men as much as they could and could only communicate with their troops through an interpreter. Tolerance of things Indian gradually gave way to a weary contempt, as William Hodson, a flamboyant intelligence officer and commander of irregular cavalry, observed a few years before the Mutiny:

At the age at which officers become colonels and majors, not one in fifty is able to stand the wear and tear of Indian service. They become still more worn in mind than in body. All elasticity is gone; all energy and enterprise worn out; they become, after a fortnight's campaign, a burden to themselves, an annoyance to those under them, and a terror to every one but the enemy!

Yet the weakening bonds between the British officer and the sepoy paled in significance against a more profound threat to Indian culture: the gradual imposition of Western ideas and attitudes, the introduction of which was meant to sweep away centuries of superstition and heathen practices. The greatest liberal thinker of the 19th century, John Stuart Mill, strongly advocated the application of British culture and institutions abroad for the betterment of 'backward' societies. In his *Considerations on Representative Government* (1861), he argued that the colonies could enjoy the benefits of Britain's sophistication:

first, a better government: more complete security of property; moderate taxes; a more permanent ... tenure of land. Secondly, improvement of the public intelligence; the decay of usages or superstitions which interfere with the effective implementation of industry; and the growth of mental activity, making the people alive to new objects of desire. Thirdly, the introduction of foreign arts ... and the introduction of foreign capital, which renders the increase of production no longer exclusively dependent on the thrift or providence of the inhabitants themselves, while it places before them a stimulating example.

On this basis British reformers set out to eradicate 'backward', even 'barbaric' practices, which to them belonged to a degenerate culture, not to an enlightened, God-fearing civilization. In the early 19th century the principal objects of attack were *thagi* (known to contemporaries as 'thuggee', and the origin of the word 'thug'), the practice by which gangs, acting in the name of the goddess Kali, ritually murdered by strangulation unsuspecting travellers on the roads; female infanticide; and the most reviled of all customs, *sati* (spelled 'suttee' by contemporaries), in which a Hindu widow committed suicide by throwing herself into the flames of her husband's funeral pyre as an act of marital fidelity. British authorities not only stamped out *thagi* and abolished *sati*, but legalized the re-marriage of widows, and introduced British-style courts, property laws, new roads, canals and the electric telegraph, all to the consternation of a wide section of conservative Indian society. 'Progress' clearly lay in the eye of the beholder.

By imposing British standards of conduct and law, administrators cast themselves as (doubtless well-intentioned) modernizers, apparently far-sighted, yet often oblivious to the potential dangers inherent in tampering with the religious and cultural practices of a civilization more ancient than their own. There were those who cautioned against Western interference in the cultural and religious sensitivities of the Indians. A generation before the Mutiny, Lieutenant-Colonel William Playfaire had written to the governor-general's secretary, warning that the abolition of *sati* might lead to fatal consequences:

Any order of government prohibiting the practice would create a most alarming sensation throughout the native army; they would consider it an interference with their customs and religion amounting to an abandonment of those principles which have hitherto guided government in its conduct towards them. Such a feeling once excited, there is no possibility of predicting what might happen. It might break out in some parts of the army in open rebellion ...

The fact that no mutiny occurred then may very well have lulled the authorities into the mistaken belief that Indians would tolerate, if not welcome, reform, without adverse reaction. When, however, religion appeared to come under direct threat, matters grew considerably more serious. The fears amongst many Indians that the British were bent on replacing Indian religions with Christianity may be identified as one of the principal causes of the Mutiny.

That is not to say that religious tension was a longstanding feature of British colonial rule in India. Quite the contrary: in the 18th century the British had built their empire upon an amoral pursuit of territory, power, natural resources and trade, largely without interest in altering foreign cultures, wherever on the globe they might happen

to live. In India specifically, despite the increasingly evangelical movement at home, the East India Company had actively discouraged the propagation of Christianity; rather it operated on the basis of mutual toleration – if only for pragmatic reasons.

Business was its *raison d'être*; the notion of trying to alter Indian culture or religion, whether through the propagation of Christianity or by other means, made no financial sense, for it threatened an existing order which consistently generated healthy, sometimes extravagant, profits for the expatriate business community.

In short, so long as Anglo-Indian relations remained on a footing favourable to business, no reason existed for challenging the status quo. Indeed, Company rules expressly banned chaplains from preaching amongst Indians; they were to confine themselves to the spiritual welfare of the European community alone. Missionaries were allowed into India, but only in limited numbers and in a restricted area. In 1808, Robert Dundas, the President of the Board of Control, which administered Indian affairs from London, expressed the government's view on the spreading of the Christian faith:

We are very far from being averse to the introduction of Christianity into India ... but nothing could be more unwise than any imprudent or injudicious attempt to induce it by means which should irritate and alarm their religious prejudices ... It is desirable that the knowledge of Christianity should be imparted to the native, but the means to be used for that end shall only be such as shall be free from any political danger or alarm ... Our paramount power imposes upon us the necessity to protect the native inhabitants in the free and undisturbed possession of their religious opinions.

When, however, in 1813, the charter of the East India Company came up for renewal, the rights of missionaries to operate in India expanded exponentially, sowing the seeds of discord. Hundreds of petitions were presented to Parliament, their signatories roused by evangelical spirit, calling for the end of restrictions on missionary activity in India.

Coffee party at a military station in India, c.1850.
British soldiers posted to India in the mid-19th century
increasingly held themselves aloof from the sepoys by
deliberate segregation, in sharp contrast to the habits of
their Georgian forebears, who had prided themselves on
establishing a solid paternal relationship with their troops.

The Company could not resist this torrent of
changing opinion, which found expression in
a preamble that ran thus:

*The inhabitants of the populous regions
in India which form an important portion of
the British Empire, being involved in the most
deplorable state of moral darkness, and under
the influence of the most abominable and
degrading superstitions, have a pre-eminent
claim on the most compassionate feelings
and benevolent services of British Christians.*

The increase in the number of missionaries
in India was very gradual, but by 1832 there
were 58 Church Missionary Society preachers
working on the sub-continent, with more
arriving each year.

By the 1850s a wave of Christian
revivalism had swept across Britain,
where efforts to propagate the faith abroad
had become a *cause célèbre* bordering on a
national obsession. As Macleod Wylie wrote
in *Bengal as a Field of Missions* in 1854:

*When the contrast between the influence
of a Christian and a Heathen government
is considered; when the knowledge of the
wretchedness of the people forces us to reflect
on the unspeakable blessings of millions that
would follow the extension of British rule,*

This shift in approach towards India was no conspiracy of government, but rather reflected the general aim of Christian missionary societies who took it upon themselves to bring, as they saw it, 'light' to 'dark' continents, including India.

The British Empire had for two centuries pursued trade, colonization and forcible occupation, all the while exporting British goods, capital and people. Imperialists of the post-Napoleonic era now introduced a new component: British culture and the dominant religion of the West. Profit, for once, played no part in this aspect of continued British expansion: spreading the Gospel and saving souls had become, for the British public in general and missionaries in particular, a moral imperative. As God had made the British responsible for ruling a large proportion of the world's population, it seemed natural that the country had a sacred duty to improve the lot of its subject peoples: materially, morally, and above all spiritually. The men who undertook this at times dangerous enterprise were altruistic, idealistic, highly motivated adventurers who were prepared to sacrifice everything for the sake of spreading the Word in what amounted to a new form of imperialism: evangelical imperialism.

Indian society, being feudal, itself deeply religious, and subject to an ancient caste system with no counterpart in the West, easily took offence at the enthusiasm with which missionaries sought to import their faith. High-caste Hindus – Brahmins and Rajputs in particular – viewed this as a deliberate attempt to usurp the caste system that was integral to their culture. Quite apart from the work of the missionaries themselves, the fact that regimental officers regularly preached from the Bible during troop assemblies contributed to such fears.

Those perceptive enough to detect trouble brewing naturally reported it to their superiors, only to find their claims dismissed by those who, whether through arrogance, complacency or short-sightedness, took the loyalty of sepoy troops for granted.

it is not ambition but benevolence that dictates the desire for the whole country. Where the providence of God will lead, one state after another will be delivered into his stewardship.

In sharp contrast to their more worldly predecessors, the Victorians' imperative was to redeem the world, not simply to rule it. Exploitation in the more naked sense of the 18th century gave way to a desire – indeed a compulsion – to convert heathen, primitive peoples, with India fertile ground for the conversion of lost souls. The goal was now to 'civilize' rather than simply to colonize, notwithstanding the fact that Indian culture was ancient and more sophisticated than many Britons were prepared to admit.

Opposing forces

Rebel forces

British rule on the sub-continent rested overwhelmingly on the strength of the East India Company's forces, which throughout the 18th century served under British officers as a loosely organized body of Indian mercenary troops drawn from a society which placed great stock in the military profession. By the time of the Mutiny, the three Company armies had largely become professional rather than mercenary in character, and were maintained on a Western model.

In 1857, apart from a few all-British (known to contemporaries as 'European') units, the Company's forces were composed of a mixture of Hindu, Muslim and Sikh troops, known as 'sepoys'. The number of native troops stood at 311,000, or more than seven times the number of men serving in all-British units or the regular British Army, known as 'Queen's' troops. The Company's record in the field over the previous century was an impressive one, with recent successful campaigns in Burma in the 1820s, in Sind in 1843, in Gwalior in the same year, and in the Punjab in 1845–46 and 1848–49. One of its few defeats – albeit of catastrophic proportions – occurred in 1842 when General Elphinstone's entire force was wiped out during the retreat from Kabul to Jellalabad.

Of the soldiers in the East India Company service, 80 per cent were drawn from warrior castes. Military service was inseparably bound up in religion; on the eve of battle Hindu soldiers made sacrifices or offerings to the idol of Kali, the goddess of destruction, to receive her protection and blessing. For Hindus, society was divided into four distinct classes, with specified professions for each, military service being reserved for the two highest classes, consisting of the Ksatriya, and, at the top, the Brahmin.

Men from different classes – sub-divided into numerous different castes based on racial or tribal origin, and profession – avoided close contact wherever possible, to avoid defiling their caste. This was largely overlooked in the Madras and Bombay armies for the sake of military expediency, to avoid the obvious difficulties arising out of circumstances where a soldier from a lower caste was required to issue orders to one from a higher caste. By overlooking caste differences in order to preserve the integrity of this military fraternity, troops from these armies bound themselves together in an effectively new caste – the army.

The majority of mutineers, on the other hand, originated from the Bengal Army (the largest of the Company's three armies), recruited mostly from the northern state of Oudh and other conservative princely states where the co-mingling of soldiers from different classes and castes proved more difficult and where the men were more susceptible to disaffection. Of the 123 regular, irregular and local units of the Bengal Army, 59 mutinied and 37 partially mutinied, or were disarmed or disbanded. Of those which were regular infantry, cavalry and artillery units, 50 mutinied and 33 partially mutinied. Over 60 per cent of its troops were either Brahmin or Ksatriya soldiers, the remainder consisting of recruits from other Hindu castes, or Muslims. Hindus regarded Muslims and Christians as 'untouchables'.

Most Company regiments were organized and clothed on the model of the British Army, which meant that, at least in the earlier actions of the war, both sides found themselves in the peculiar position of fighting opponents dressed and armed almost identically, and employing the same tactics. Paradoxically, some rebel units continued to wear the medals they

Sepoy troops on the march. Soldiers such as these hailed from various regions and martial castes in India, such as the Rajputs and the Gujars, the latter a migrant agricultural caste. Nevertheless, support for the mutineers was largely confined to the cities; whole swathes of the countryside remained either passive or supportive of attempts to restore British rule. (Philip Haythornthwaite)

had received in British-led campaigns against the Afghans and Sikhs, and in some cases regimental bands continued to play British tunes in action against their erstwhile allies. As the conflict developed, the mutineers tended to shed their Company uniforms and wear their accoutrements over indigenous clothing – including turbans or skull caps, and white flowing trousers (*dhoti*) – and the tight-fitting single-breasted British-style jacket was gradually replaced by a more comfortable garment.

As time passed, and mutinous soldiers mixed with civilian insurgents, the old regimental discipline and structure began to weaken, and the lack of unified command and skilful leadership put them at a distinct disadvantage in the field, even when they outnumbered their opponents by several times. The rebels were not completely bereft of competent leadership – Tantia Topi and

the Rani of Jhansi both proved inspirational and determined – but their revolt left them without an officer cadre to replace their former commanders. In weaponry, too, the mutineers stood at a disadvantage, for they continued to use the old smooth-bore Brown Bess musket, an inferior weapon to the new Enfield rifle, which enjoyed a range three times as great.

Queen's regiments and the British forces of the East India Company

British regiments in the Queen's service, often referred to as the 'British Army in India' or 'the Queen's Service in India', formed only a small minority of troops in India. On the eve of the Mutiny there should have been 26 infantry battalions or cavalry regiments stationed in India, but five had been sent to the Crimea in 1854 (of which only one was replaced), and three had been dispatched for service in Persia two years later. The total number of 'British' troops in India (i.e. Queen's regiments, all-British East India Company units, and the white officers of native regiments) stood at only 40,000,

Sepoys of the 21st Madras Native Infantry in the service of the East India Company on the march. Company soldiers were armed, organized, clothed and trained in the fashion of the British Army. (Philip Haythornthwaite)

of which about 24,000 were Queen's troops. Thus, the proportion of British to Indian troops at the start of the rebellion stood at about 1 to 7.7. As British troops were far more expensive to train and pay than their Indian counterparts (more than twice as much), in the absence of any clear sign of discontent military authorities contented themselves with disproportionately low numbers of 'white' troops, confident in the loyalty of 'native' soldiers.

In Bengal, 'British' Company forces, who were better paid than their counterparts in the British Army and received promotion by strict seniority rather than by purchase, consisted of three battalions of infantry, 66 pieces of foot artillery, 54 of horse, and garrison companies. The Bombay and Madras presidencies also had three battalions of British infantry each, but only 18 horse artillery guns each, and 33 and 44 guns in the foot artillery, respectively. At the start of the Mutiny, the Crown's forces in India (that is, Queen's regiments) numbered 18 battalions of infantry and four regiments of cavalry, though two infantry battalions and one light dragoon regiment were on service in Persia. The 19 units stationed in India were not only small in number, but unevenly distributed around the country. In the 600 miles (966km) between Calcutta and Cawnpore, one infantry battalion was based at Calcutta and one at Dinapore; one infantry battalion was at Lucknow; a single regiment of dragoon guards and a rifle battalion were based at Meerut. Only four units were stationed in the Madras and Bombay presidencies, leaving all the remaining units of the British Army in India scattered across the Punjab, in the north-west of the country, between Umballa (130 miles [209km] from Meerut) and Peshawar (400 miles [644km] to the north-west).

This distribution, while ensuring that both the North-West Frontier and the Punjab would remain quiet, nevertheless delayed the conduct of major operations to the south; specifically, Delhi could not be retaken without the arrival of reinforcements from the Punjab and Meerut. Some troops, of course, were required to remain in the Punjab and on the Afghan frontier, but others, over time, were called upon from around the Empire: those serving in Persia were recalled; three battalions came from Burma; one from Ceylon; four and half, en route to China, were diverted to India; and eventually other units arrived from other stations around the world, including Australia, the Cape Colony, Malta and of course Britain, including regiments newly returned from the Crimea. Although frequently understrength and fatigued from service, regiments fresh from Russia were in great demand to meet the emergency in India. In the course of the Mutiny, eight cavalry regiments, 47 infantry battalions, transport units, large numbers of artillery batteries, and units of the Royal Engineers were dispatched to India. By the end of the conflict almost two-thirds of the British Army – at least 15 per cent more men than had been deployed in the Crimea – were

serving on the sub-continent, though only a third of all forces participated in the main theatres of operation.

Loyal native forces

The Indian Mutiny was not a conflict solely between British and Indian soldiers; indeed, the British depended heavily on the aid provided by their Indian allies, not least because in the initial stages of the conflict it was impossible to assemble a large field army without Indian units to bolster their numbers in a theatre of operations of immense proportions. Large numbers of sepoys, mainly Sikhs and Gurkhas, remained loyal to the British cause and fought with resolution and bravery. The Gurkhas were largely drawn from Nepal, having originally fought the British in 1815, impressing them with their martial abilities. The Sikhs had only recently been defeated, and their homeland,

Lakshmi Bai, Rani of Jhansi. A widow in her thirties, as one of the two outstanding rebel leaders she became a heroine of the revolt. In battle she dressed as a man, often carrying her sword in both hands while holding the reins of her horse in her mouth. She was killed in a cavalry skirmish near Gwalior in June 1858. (Author's collection)

British troops at the camp outside Delhi. Notwithstanding the obvious advantages of superior range and accuracy bestowed by the new Enfield rifle, much of the fighting in the Mutiny was conducted at close quarters, and thus victory in the field may in part be attributed more to superior British discipline and bayonet-practice than to firepower. (Author's collection)

the Punjab, annexed in 1849. Anxious to regain their independence, they might have been expected to be natural enemies of the British. Yet in fact the two sides had gained considerable mutual respect for one another's fighting qualities, and British rule over the Punjab was widely regarded as competent and fair. Antipathy arose, however, between the Sikhs and the occupying regiments from Bengal, whose high-caste sepoys viewed the Sikhs as unclean and uncivilized, while the Sikhs – based on their recent conduct in the field – viewed the martial abilities of the sepoys with contempt. Thus, in 1857, far from taking advantage of the opportunity to regain their independence, the Sikhs saw the chance to avenge themselves on fellow Indians.

A small contingent of the Bengal Army remained under British authority, but most of the Indian units consisted of newly formed corps of irregular cavalry, and infantry from the Punjab, plus Sikh infantry and cavalry and Gurkhas. Many British and Anglo-Indian auxiliary units, mostly mounted, were hastily raised, later to be disbanded after the Mutiny.

The Bombay Army, which with the exception of two regiments remained loyal, contributed considerably to success, together with troops from Hyderabad, in the campaign of 1858 in central India. The Madras Army proved itself entirely reliable, and, though it played only a minor role in central India, sent some troops to fight in Oudh. While most of the Bengal Army mutinied, three irregular cavalry regiments, and four of infantry, plus contingents of three other units, remained loyal, as did three Gurkha battalions, several units of Sikhs, and various other irregular units, both infantry and artillery. The most important element of loyal troops, however, came from the Punjab, whose Sikh troops kept watch not only along the North-West Frontier, but also in the major operations in northern India. These consisted of five cavalry regiments, ten infantry battalions, and a corps of guides. As more recruits presented themselves, new irregular cavalry units were formed and more than a dozen battalions of infantry. Sikhs were not the only recruits: Punjabi Muslims, Gurkhas, Pathans, Afghans and Baluchis, who had no ethnic or religious connection with the predominantly Hindu sepoys, also comprised the loyal Indian forces.

Unredressed grievances

Much has been made of the greased cartridges of the new Enfield rifle as the cause of the Mutiny. However, a general feeling of dissatisfaction had been growing in the ranks of the sepoy regiments for some time. During Lord Dalhousie's administration as Governor-General (1848–56), the terms of enlistment underwent a fundamental change: sepoys were to be enlisted for general service only, which meant that, once discharged, the men would receive no pension. Thereafter, strong suspicions circulated amongst those men recruited before the change in policy that the same regulations would eventually be applied to them. Such anxieties were compounded by the fact that sepoys of the Bengal Army were paid less than their counterparts in the armies of Madras and Bombay.

Threats to pay were compounded by anxieties concerning promotion, for which an Indian soldier's prospects were poor. Whereas, in the days of Clive, sepoy regiments contained fewer than half a dozen British officers, with many positions of responsibility open to Indians, well before the Mutiny the proportion of British officers had been increased, with the ability of Indians to rise through the ranks correspondingly diminished. Sir Henry Lawrence, chief commissioner for Oudh noted that:

The sepoy feels that we cannot do without him; and yet the highest reward that a sepoy can obtain ... is about one hundred pounds a year without a prospect of a brighter career for his son. Surely this is not [an] inducement to offer to a foreign soldier for special fidelity and long service.

Lawrence thought it unreasonable to expect 'that the energetic and aspiring among *immense* military masses should like our ... arrogation to ourselves ... of *all* authority and

emolument ...'. In remarking on the unfair system of promotion, he obliquely referred to the possibility of revolt, writing that

We ought either to disband our army or open our posts of honour and emolument to its aspiring members. We act contrary to common sense, and in neglect of the lessons of history, in considering that the present system can lead to anything but a convulsion. We are lucky in its having lasted so long.

Various Indian princes harboured grievances against the British for the implementation of a new policy of annexation, and saw mutiny as an opportunity to regain lost power and territory. Under Dalhousie's administration, according to the newly prescribed 'doctrine of lapse', the Company began annexing any Indian state in which the ruler died without a natural heir. This was applied in the cases of Nagpur and Jhansi, and naturally left a feeling of unease amongst Indian princes whose sovereignty rested on centuries of hereditary right. The introduction for the first time of a land-title system, resulting in the confiscation of thousands of estates and small plots, provoked widespread anger.

In February 1856 the Company annexed the badly governed and corrupt kingdom of Oudh (now Uttar Pradesh); Oudh stretched across a large area of northern India containing a predominantly Hindu population, ruled by the last independent Muslim dynasty in India. The annexation played a crucial part in the disaffection of the Bengal Army: perhaps as many as 75,000 of whose troops came from Oudh. Many inhabitants regarded the annexation as an illegitimate political act by which their nawab, Wajid Ali, was deposed and the army of 60,000 men disbanded after the payment of token gratuities – a clear sign that the Company was bent on territorial

LEFT Indian prince posing. While by 1857 most of India was under direct British control, there still remained a decreasing number of semi-independent states under princes and maharajahs receiving British 'protection', such as Gwalior and Hyderabad. (British Library)

annexation for its own sake. Other princes, looking with dismay upon the fate of Oudh, quite understandably considered their own territories under threat.

This had important religious and practical consequences, for, with the disappearance of Oudh as an independent state, the higher classes of soldiers were deprived of rights and privileges at court once granted by the old regime, thus losing a degree of the prestige formerly held by the military profession. It was precisely this institution, the army, which helped maintain social cohesion, and with its status in the social order threatened, general disquiet was perhaps inevitable.

Three-quarters of the soldiers of the Bengal Army recruited from Oudh were high-caste Hindus (i.e. Brahmins and Rajputs), often the sons of landowners on whose support British rule depended, who resented the introduction of the new

General Service Enlistment Act (1856) whose regulations, notwithstanding the sepoys' strong objections, required them to serve outside India if military circumstances should prove necessary. Quite apart from drawing soldiers away from their native regions and families, taking them across the sea would deprive them of their caste. Whereas in previous years the Company had offered a bounty for those serving abroad, which could pay for rites of purification, this was withdrawn as of July 1856. If required, sepoys would have to serve in Afghanistan, Burma or farther afield. Recruitment suffered as a result, which led to fears that British authorities would in turn resort to accepting men from low castes in order to meet their quotas, or even accept untouchables.

Signs that trouble was afoot occurred with the mysterious appearance of *chapattis*

BELOW The gatehouse of Barrackpore House, Calcutta, one of the official residences of Lord Canning, the Governor-General of India. Canning supervised the administration of the Raj as carried out by the East India Company. (British Library)

(unleavened bread or cakes, generally eaten by the poor and the soldiery), which began to be circulated amongst the populace throughout north-western India at the beginning of 1857. Messengers bearing chapattis arrived in villages at night, giving instructions that more should be baked to be distributed to other villages as a form of chain-letter. The meaning of this practice was unclear, but it was at the time believed to be a premonition or portent of a momentous event; to some it represented the beginning of the end of British rule on the sub-continent – a notion reinforced by an old prophecy of unknown origin, which stated that British rule would cease forever during the centenary of the battle of Plassey, i.e. in 1857.

To this day no one quite knows the meaning behind these events. What is certain is that they coincided with the most significant immediate provocation for mutiny: the introduction of greased cartridges for use with the new Enfield rifle. The majority of the Company's infantry regiments had by this time ceased to use the old Brown Bess musket and were armed with the 1842 pattern percussion musket. In 1856, however, the Company introduced the new Enfield rifle, whose greater accuracy and range over the musket had recently proven itself in the Crimea. The ammunition supplied for the Enfield consisted of an entirely new form of cartridge and a new loading drill. The cartridge consisted of a cardboard cylinder containing gunpowder and a lead ball. To open the cartridge, which contained grease at its lower end, the soldier either tore, or more commonly bit, off a twist of paper which held the contents of powder and ball inside. Some of the powder was poured down the barrel, the remainder being used to prime the charge. The cartridge was then rammed home, the process facilitated by the grease smeared on the paper.

Herein lay the problem. It is thought that in January 1857, a low-caste ammunition labourer at the small arms arsenal at Dum-Dum, near Calcutta, informed a Brahmin sepoy that the grease used in the manufacture of the cartridges contained a mixture of cow and pig fat – and was therefore an abomination both to Muslims, who regarded pigs as unclean, and to Hindus, who venerated the cow. The imposition of the new cartridges was believed to serve the cunning function of defiling those who came in contact with the grease, so subverting their religion and enforcing on them Christianity, as any soldier who so defiled himself would lose caste. British authorities declared their intention to investigate the matter of the greased cartridges, but either this news was not properly disseminated amongst the troops, or the sepoys did not trust that a proper solution would be found.

While no conspiracy existed on the part of British authorities to subvert the troops' religion, in all likelihood the grease did contain animal fat, for the regulations concerning the manufacture of the cartridges did not stipulate the type to be used, and contractors would naturally be inclined to use the least expensive variety, tallow, which was based on animal fat. The new cartridges were, in fact, never issued to the troops, and after some consideration that sepoys should be allowed to grease their own cartridges with a substance of their choice, the Government directed that the grease used should be prepared only from mutton fat and wax. But it was too little, too late, and either out of lack of understanding or lack of sympathy, military authorities failed to consult the troops or sufficiently reassure them before the damaging rumour had spread. The absence of any evidence of malice or conspiracy on the part of the British – who largely viewed this as a trivial issue – is an irrelevance: the sepoys' existing suspicions of a plot to enforce Christianity upon them remained. Their greatest fears now realized, it was only a matter of time before discontent bubbled over into outright violence.

The potential for such violence ought not to have been lost on British authorities. Mutiny had broken out before, in the summer of 1806 at Vellore, when new dress regulations abolished the sepoys' right to wear beards or markings indicating their caste, and introduced a new style of turban. To make matters worse, what to Company officials appeared a matter of no consequence – the issuance of a new cockade made of cow or pig hide – was in fact fundamentally offensive to Hindus and Muslims, and exacerbated existing grievances about such practical matters as pay and conditions of service. Half a century later the lessons of Vellore had been either forgotten or ignored, for the most fundamental cause of the mutiny of 1806 and that of 1857 was the same: British attempts to interfere in Indian culture were perceived as a plot to Christianize the country.

The Mutiny begins

The first signs of mutiny occurred in January 1857, when the 34th Native Infantry at Barrackpore showed signs of discontent. The following month, on 26 February, the same regiment disaffected the 19th Native Infantry at Berhampore, as a result of which the government in Calcutta ordered the 84th Foot from Rangoon. It arrived on 20 March and marched to the area around Barrackpore, where the 19th Native Infantry was being conducted to be disarmed and disbanded. On 29 March, however, Mungal Pandy, a private of the 34th Native Infantry (his name subsequently gave rise to the British use of the nickname 'Pandy' to describe mutineers in general), loaded his musket and declared that he would shoot the first British officer he encountered. Lieutenant Baugh, the regiment's adjutant, on learning of this, rode out to the parade ground. As he approached, Pandy fired at him, wounding his horse, and bringing down both mount and rider. Though armed, Baugh almost certainly would have been killed had it not been for the intervention of his Indian orderly, who saved his life by seizing Pandy just as he had managed to reload his musket. Several other men of the 34th prevented officers from assisting Baugh, and the sepoys did not desist until

Major-General Hearsey rode up, threatening to shoot anyone who refused to obey his orders.

What many British observers believed to be an isolated affair in fact precipitated further outbreaks of violence. On 30 March, the 19th Native Infantry arrived at Barraset, 8 miles (nearly 13km) from Barrackpore, where they were received by a deputation from the 34th who proposed that the two regiments should murder their officers, proceed to Barrackpore at night, to be joined by the 2nd and 34th, set fire to the British residences, surprise and overwhelm the Queen's regiments, seize the artillery, and then proceed to Calcutta. The 19th Native Infantry refused to join this conspiracy, entered Barrackpore without incident the next morning and gave up their weapons to the 84th Foot. The 19th then marched to their cantonments and were discharged, they being the first native regiment to be disarmed and disbanded as a result of the disturbances. Mungal Pandy was tried and executed, together with another soldier of the 34th, who had commanded the guard on 29 March. Nothing further occurred by way of prosecutions, and during the whole of April the government in Calcutta remained idle, taking no steps to avert the possibility of further acts of mutiny, and remaining largely ignorant of events.

The next disturbance occurred in Oudh, where at Lucknow the 7th Native Irregulars, on learning of the disbanding of the 19th Native Infantry, appeared to show signs of disobedience. The British Commissioner there, Sir Henry Lawrence, having intercepted a letter from the 7th Irregulars to another sepoy unit declaring its desire to mutiny, immediately ordered his garrison, including a battery of eight guns with a British crew, to assemble around the men of the 7th. They called upon the 7th to lay down its weapons as the gunners stood holding lit portfires. The men of the 7th obeyed the command, those deemed responsible for conspiracy to mutiny were arrested, and the remainder were discharged. For the moment, at least, all remained calm in Oudh.

War without mercy

Peace was short-lived, however. Unrest was simmering at a garrison town in the Bengal Presidency about 40 miles (64km) north of Delhi, Meerut, an important junction on the Grand Trunk Road and the home of a large garrison consisting of both Company troops and Queen's regiments. On 24 April all but five men of a contingent of the 3rd Light Cavalry refused to assemble for carbine practice. The 85 troopers who had disobeyed their orders were brought before a court-martial, and sentenced to ten years' imprisonment with hard labour. On 9 May, the sentences were read out on parade in the presence of the entire garrison, consisting of British regiments with loaded weapons and native regiments without. In an act of public humiliation, the convicted men were stripped of their uniforms, shackled and led off to jail. The regiment contained many veterans with long-standing service to the Company, yet appeals for mercy were dismissed.

On the following night, Sunday 10 May, while the British were attending church, the 11th and 20th Native Infantry began to assemble in a boisterous manner, goaded by a mob from the local bazaar. Their British officers immediately appeared to restore order in their ranks, but no sooner had Colonel Finnis appeared on the scene than he was shot in the back while shouting at the 20th. Toppling from his horse, he was cut to pieces by the enraged sepoys, whose conduct initiated a general slaughter. The men of the 3rd made rapidly for

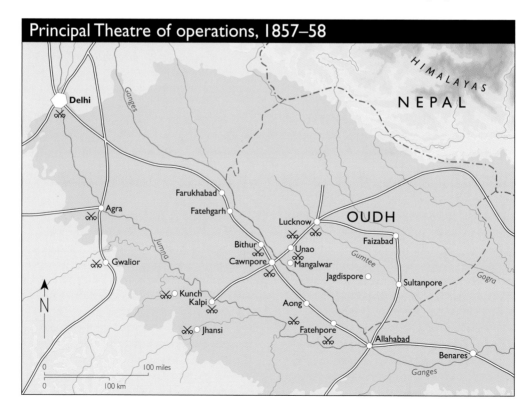

Principal Theatre of operations, 1857–58

the jail, broke down the gates, released their comrades and all other prisoners, and proceeded to plunder and burn the British bungalows in a frenzy of destruction and murder. British officers who tried to intervene were shot down or bayoneted, including the colonel of the 11th. An indiscriminate slaughter of all Europeans, regardless of sex or age, began. The women and children, who tried to hide where they could, largely in the gardens, were set upon and shot or stabbed. Private Joseph Bowater described the events thus:

There was a sudden rising ... a rush to the horses, a swift swaddling, a gallop to the gaol ... a breaking open of the gates, and a setting free, not only of the mutineers who had been court-martialled, but also of more than a thousand cut-throats and scoundrels of every sort. Simultaneously, the native infantry fell upon and massacred their British officers, and butchered the women and children in a way that you cannot describe. Gaolbirds, bazaar riff-raff, and Sepoys – all the disaffected natives in Meerut – blood-mad, set about their work with diabolical cruelty, and, to crown their task, they fired every building they came across.

Mutineers shooting their commanding officer, Colonel Platt of the 11th Native Infantry, on 10 May 1857. While obvious signs of discontent in the Bengal Army were gradually surfacing in the 1850s, most military authorities failed to forecast impending disaster. (Philip Haythornthwaite)

The military response was too slow, in spite of the fact that the Meerut garrison, under General Hewitt – paralysed by indecision – consisted of the 60th Rifles, the 6th Dragoon Guards, a troop of horse artillery, and 500 artillerymen. About 2,000 men in total, all were billeted too far away to enable them to intervene in time. By the time the Dragoon Guards reached the scene at nightfall the carnage was over and the buildings were smoking ruins. At the parade ground they found the 60th Rifles and artillery already assembled, but the mutineers had already left for Delhi, 36 miles (58km) away. Hewitt made a second error in failing to pursue the rebels with the cavalry and horse artillery, thus losing an opportunity to defeat them before they could reach Delhi. Instead he merely ordered a reconnaissance and rejected a suggestion that a patrol seize the bridge over the Jumna.

Elsewhere, the mutiny spread rapidly throughout the Bengal Army and across the

Flight from Delhi. Small numbers of European civilians managed to escape certain death at the hands of the mutineers by the desperate expedient of wandering through jungles and swimming across rivers in search of safety at a British station. (Author's collection)

north, affecting Delhi, Benares, Allahabad and Cawnpore and much of the area east towards Calcutta. Some garrison commanders were able to disarm their native regiments before rebellion reached them such as at Agra, Lahore, Peshawar and Mardan, while others, showing more caution on the basis that mere disaffection would not result in violence, met the same fate as the troops at Meerut. The pattern of soldiers running amok, sometimes involving local civilian mobs, and indiscriminately murdering Europeans, was repeated across many towns, where small garrisons fought to protect themselves and their wives and children.

That the Mutiny was not an organized uprising is confirmed by the fact that both sides were caught unprepared. Those Company regiments which mutinied did so at different times, with no coordination between units. Thus, the revolt came as a complete surprise, and Company authorities sought to meet the emergency with the small

numbers of reliable troops at their disposal, these being limited to Queen's and all-British Company regiments, plus whatever native troops could be presumed to be loyal.

While the fate of the many small garrisons, scattered across Bengal and elsewhere, which had to fend for themselves as best they could cannot for reasons of space find a place in this work, it is perhaps sufficient to observe that those not immediately wiped out held on with grim determination, completely unaware of the extent of the rebellion or of their own prospect of relief. At least one, however, cannot go without notice. Perhaps the most celebrated instance took place in a billiard-hall at Arrah, near Dinapore, where 16 British and Eurasian officials and their servants, together with 45 loyal Sikhs, fortified the building and held out against constant attacks until relief finally arrived on 3 August.

The siege of Delhi, June–September 1857

Notwithstanding the obvious initial disadvantages under which they laboured –

Sir John Lawrence, Chief Commissioner of the recently annexed Punjab. Within days of hearing of the outbreak of mutiny he took firm action, disarming suspect sepoy regiments, securing arsenals and treasuries, occupying important strategic positions and executing mutinous leaders. In addition to securing the Punjab, he generously dispatched every regiment he could spare to aid the besieging force at Delhi, despite the risk of unrest in his own province. (Philip Haythornthwaite)

namely numerical inferiority, logistical unpreparedness, the wide dispersal of their troops and the need to secure the Punjab and Afghan frontier while simultaneously confronting the major rebel concentrations elsewhere – British authorities had three objectives from the outset: first, having identified Delhi as the seat of the rebellion, to assume the offensive and retake it from the mutineers and their civilian supporters; secondly, to try to relieve other important British garrison cities which were under siege, most importantly Lucknow and, to a lesser extent, Cawnpore; and, thirdly, to disrupt the mutineers' ability to concentrate their forces

and so deprive them wherever possible of the advantage of numerical superiority. Herein lay the fundamental problem which faced the British from the start: how to concentrate their scattered forces in order to pursue an ambitious strategy, while at the same time making only limited use of Indian troops whose loyalty they suspected. Those of the Bengal Army were clearly unreliable, while the intentions of those from the Bombay and Madras armies were as yet uncertain. Consequently, the only troops immediately available and of unquestionable fidelity were the British regiments of the East India Company and the handful of units of the British Army then in India. There was no pool of reserves in India itself, and reinforcements could not be expected to arrive for months. Meanwhile, the principal surviving British posts had to cope as best they could: Sir Henry Lawrence at Lucknow; Sir John Lawrence at Lahore, in the Punjab; Sir Hugh Wheeler at Cawnpore; and John Colvin, the Lieutenant-Governor of the North-West Provinces, at Agra. Lord Canning, the Governor-General, was busy with administration in Calcutta, appealing to London for more troops.

Meanwhile, having marched all night, the 11th and 20th regiments of the Bengal Native Infantry, and the 3rd Bengal Cavalry, arrived on the morning of 11 May in Delhi, where they were joined by the 38th, 54th and 74th Native Infantry. In the course of the day these six regiments took control of the city – which did not contain a single British regiment – and hunted down and massacred all the Europeans they could find. Some remained in hiding in the city, while others, in small groups, offered futile resistance, penned up in offices and houses. Those fortunate enough to escape made their way through jungles and over streams and rivers. In one of the great epics of the Mutiny, Lieutenant George Willoughby, Commissary of Ordnance, with eight others, desperately defended the massive Delhi magazine, blowing it up at the last moment

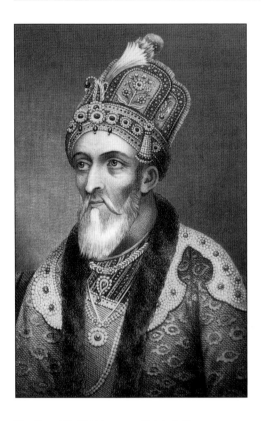

The King of Delhi. Living on an East India Company pension, the 82-year-old Bahadur Shah II, the last Mughal emperor, exercised no political power until the rebels declared him their leader. He was probably not complicit in the actions which precipitated the Mutiny, and took up his role unwillingly. (Philip Haythornthwaite)

to prevent it falling into the hands of the mutineers as they attempted to scale the walls. Most of the defenders and a large number of rebels were killed, and much of the ammunition destroyed, but a considerable supply remained undamaged, and this and a large number of guns passed into the rebels' possession.

Once the city fell under their control, the mutineers looted shops and the houses of the wealthy, and even robbed Indians trying to cross the Jumna by the bridge of boats on the east side of the city. Although they had no proper command structure, within a few days they managed to restore order, put the city into a state of defence, and acclaim Bahadur Shah II, a feeble octogenarian and last heir of the Mughal Empire, their figurehead king, thus giving

the rebellion the focus of a single leader acceptable to both Hindus and Muslims. Amidst the cheers of their comrades, freshly arrived groups of mutineers and dissident civilians continued to converge on the city, steadily arriving from Umballa, Agra and many other towns and provinces.

As the days passed, the rebel garrison, led by the king's eldest son, Mirza Mughal, grew, so that any British force wishing to assault the place would have to contend with overwhelming numbers of defenders. Moreover, as there were no British forces in or around Delhi, the rebels had time to consolidate their position, which, in addition to the city itself, included the ridge outside the city walls and the former British cantonment behind it. It was indeed a strong position, though in concentrating their forces in Delhi the rebels failed to make any concerted effort, while the opportunity still presented itself, to eliminate what remained of British power in northern India.

Thus, the initiative passed to the British, who seized it with alacrity. The recapture of Delhi became the paramount British objective, for as the historical capital of the Mughal Empire and symbolic of the bygone days of indigenous rule, the city served as a rallying-point for the mutineers and those disaffected with colonial rule. Major-General Sir Henry Barnard, commander of forces at Umballa, 130 miles (209km) north of Delhi, was the first senior officer in a position to react to the revolt, having received a telegraph message on the afternoon of 11 May from Meerut via Delhi, notifying him of the catastrophes occurring at those places. Barnard immediately dispatched an aide de camp to the hill station at Simla, to which the telegraph had not yet been extended, to summon the 69-year-old General Sir George Anson, the Commander-in-Chief in India.

Anson, a veteran of Waterloo who had seen no action since, left Simla on the 14th and arrived at Umballa early on the following morning. The two generals had to develop a plan in the context of limited resources and various disadvantages. The magazines at

Siege of Delhi

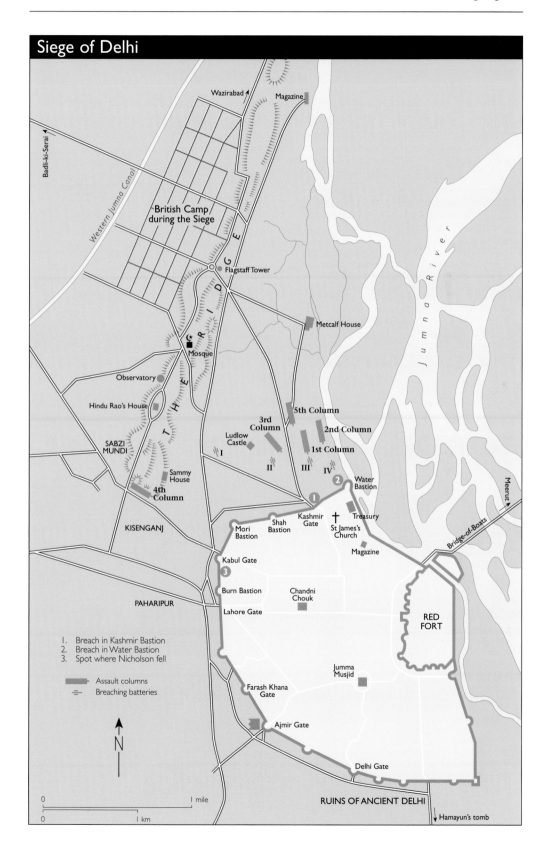

1. Breach in Kashmir Bastion
2. Breach in Water Bastion
3. Spot where Nicholson fell

Assault columns
Breaching batteries

N

0   1 mile
0   1 km

RUINS OF ANCIENT DELHI

Umballa were nearly empty of stores and ammunition; the siege gun park – without which no serious operations could be mounted against Delhi – was a considerable distance from Umballa; the artillery wagons were in the depot at Phillaur; the heat of the season would make rapid marching for the

Troops hastening from Umballa. The force assembled by General Anson consisted of the 9th Lancers, the 75th Foot, batteries of Royal Horse Artillery and two regiments of sepoys, one of which mutinied and left for Delhi, while the other was disbanded. (British Library)

3,000 available Anglo-Indian troops extremely difficult; and the commissariat was woefully short of vehicles and animals to pull both men and supplies. Notwithstanding all these difficulties, small detachments from many different posts were summoned to unite as a single column, known as the Delhi Field Force.

Regaining the initiative for the British, Anson then set off immediately with the intention of depriving the enemy of the focus of their rebellion and defeating them

in detail. In the course of the march, one of two Native Infantry regiments mutinied and made off for Delhi, while the other was disarmed, leaving Anson with only regular British Army and all-British East India Company units with which to fight.
In the event, the strain of events took a heavy toll on him, and he died of cholera on 27 May, to be succeeded in command by Major-General Barnard, who was joined by the remnant of the garrison at Meerut under Colonel Archdale Wilson.

On 8 June, in an attempt to stop the numerically inferior British force from reaching Delhi, 30,000 rebels with 30 guns established an entrenched position at Badli-ki-Serai, 5 miles (8km) north-west of the city. Wilson drove them off and established himself on a 2-mile (just over 3km-) long feature known as the Ridge which ran north to south, overlooking the north-west walls of Delhi. In a shortsighted gesture to alert the rebels as to the fate that awaited them, British troops burned the former sepoy barracks, thus leaving themselves without adequate shelter during the hottest months of the year.

The limited water supply also posed problems, for the mutineers had poisoned the cantonment wells by throwing bodies down them, and the waters of the nearby Jumna were undrinkable. To the west of the Ridge, however, the Western Jumna Canal provided an adequate source, and also provided some protection against an attack from the rear. While the Ridge itself stood 40ft (12m) above the surrounding terrain, it consisted largely of barren rock and thus provided no earth with which to construct field fortifications. Dotted about the Ridge, however, were a number of substantially built structures which British engineers soon fortified, including a mansion known as Hindu Rao's House, a tower and a ruined mosque. Between the Ridge and the city stood a stretch of no-man's land in which sat other buildings, walls, gardens and thick vegetation, all of which could be used by the rebels as staging points for sorties against the British position.

On the face of it, Delhi's defences appeared formidable, consisting of 7 miles (11km) of thick 24ft- (7.3m-) high walls with bastions mounting heavy artillery, surrounded on all sides but that facing the Jumna by a 20ft- (6m-) deep and 25ft- (7.6m-) wide ditch. Ten gates gave access to the city, with three of these – the Kashmir, Kabul and Lahore Gates – facing the Ridge.

Thus, the British position, at least at the outset, was somewhat farcical, for Barnard's force of 2,300 infantry, 600 cavalry and 22 field guns could not possibly storm a walled city, defended by several hundred pieces of ordnance, and reckoned to contain as many as 40,000 rebel troops. In consideration of such formidable odds, it is scarcely surprising that no sooner had they ensconced themselves on the Ridge than the British regarded themselves more as the besieged than the besiegers, a view confirmed by the constant and determined attacks which the rebels began to mount from the city. Each sortie was repulsed in turn with heavy losses to the enemy and moderate, though mounting, cost to the beleaguered defenders, who grimly refused to be dislodged. Meanwhile, other British columns were en route to relieve the cities of Cawnpore and Lucknow, both of which contained large British garrisons and civilian occupants.

Outside Delhi, one thing was clear: despite the urgency of an assault recommended by the chief engineer, there was no possibility of retaking the city until sufficient reinforcements, including a siege train, arrived. There was nothing for the British to do but hold their position and wait. Meanwhile, the rebels continued to bolster their garrison inside Delhi, including a sizeable force from Bareilly led by an artillery officer named Bakht Khan, who persuaded the king to appoint him commander of the city. When Barnard died from cholera on 5 July, command passed to Major-General Thomas Reed, who himself resigned after only 12 days as a result of ill health, to be succeeded by Sir Archdale Wilson, who received the temporary rank of major-general.

BELOW Fusiliers bringing captured guns into their camp outside Delhi. Despite mounting countless forays and sorties from the city between June and August, the rebels consistently failed to dislodge the besiegers. (British Library)

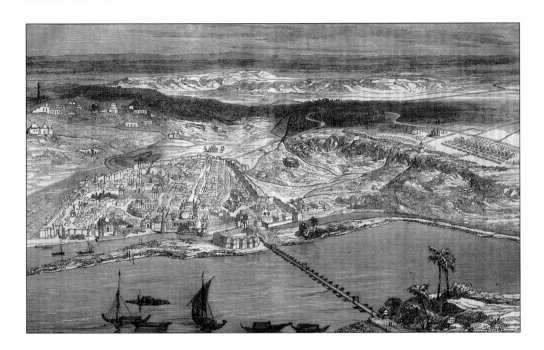

ABOVE Delhi, the ancient Mughal capital, which became the rallying point of the Mutiny. Immediately recognizing that the city's capture would signal the beginning of the end of the revolt, British troops laid siege to the place for three months, fighting an exhausting battle of attrition in which they fended off repeated attacks by the mutineers before reinforcements and heavy artillery finally arrived. (Author's collection)

Reinforcements gradually arrived from the Punjab and elsewhere, though these only maintained the force at static levels in light of the daily losses resulting from combat, heatstroke and disease, above all cholera and dysentery. Nevertheless, by the beginning of July the Delhi Field Force had grown to approximately 6,600 men – adequate numbers to fend off regular enemy attacks, but still insufficient to mount a credible attack on the walls of Delhi. At last, on 14 August, a highly mobile force known as the Moveable Column, consisting of three Punjabi cavalry regiments and seven Punjabi infantry battalions under Brigadier-General John Nicholson, reached the Ridge. Nicholson showed himself far more inspirational and charismatic than Wilson, and his personal presence contributed considerably to bolstering the besiegers' morale.

Halt on the line of march. British infantry rest by the roadside as elephants bearing mountain artillery and their crews carry on ahead. (British Library)

Enthusiastically received though these troops were, the heavy siege train, pulled by elephants, was still en route, making slow progress. When intelligence of this reached Bakht Khan, he dispatched a force of about 6,000 mutineers to intercept the convoy. Wilson's spies inside Delhi alerted him to the fact, and on 25 August Nicholson, with 2,500 men and 16 guns, discovered the rebels at Najafghar, about 16 miles (26km) from Delhi. In an hour's fighting the rebels were put to flight, leaving 800 dead and all their artillery and baggage on the field, at a cost to Nicholson of 25 killed and 70 wounded. Now realizing that their hold on the city might be temporary, the mutineers sent an envoy to the British camp on the 30th, offering terms. These were peremptorily refused: the British were in no mood to compromise with those responsible for the deaths of women and children.

At last, on 4 September, the siege train, assembled from the ordnance and stores at Phillaur and Ferozepore, together with Sikh sappers and miners, began to arrive on the Ridge. Now armed with 22 heavy guns

and mortars, plus a thousand rounds of ammunition, the Delhi Field Force possessed more than enough firepower to reduce the walls of Delhi to rubble. Yet Wilson, concerned at the still very real prospect of failure in the face of 40,000 rebels, showed great reluctance to prepare for an assault. But Nicholson, his chief engineer and other officers pointed out that the likelihood of receiving further troops and guns was low: Anglo-Indian forces had reached their peak strength, and the time had come to strike.

Troops duly occupied no-man's land without much difficulty, for after their sorties the mutineers withdrew back into the safety of the city. Under cover of darkness, gabions, fascines, gun platforms and other equipment, prepared beforehand, were brought forward by camels and bullocks, followed later by the guns. Those preparing the batteries, mostly Indian labourers, suffered heavy casualties, but by the morning of 8 September the first battery, positioned 700 yards (640m) from the Mori Bastion at the north-west corner of the city, began the bombardment, dividing its fire between the Mori Bastion and the Kashmir Bastion. The rebels replied in kind, and launched fierce sorties against the growing number of batteries appearing to their front, but the defenders consistently drove them off.

By nightfall, the Mori Bastion consisted of a heap of rubble and dismounted guns. At the same time, a second battery issued fire against the Kashmir Bastion and the curtain wall between it and the Water Bastion. A third battery, positioned within 200 yards (183m) of the walls, targeted the Water Bastion itself.

Formidable though Delhi's stone masonry was, it was also old, and could not sustain the fire of modern artillery. In the course of a few days great heaps of shattered stone filled the ditch below and by 13 September breaches large enough for infantry to make an assault practicable had been made. Wilson knew he had but one chance to take the city, for failure could prove catastrophic to the whole campaign to re-establish British authority in India. An all-out assault, conducted by 6,000 British and Indian troops organized in five columns under Nicholson's overall command, was ordered for dawn on the following morning.

At great risk to the whole enterprise, every available man was to be thrown into the cauldron, with the Ridge left in the hands of only a handful of cavalry and guns, plus the sick and wounded. Column No. 1, under Nicholson, was to enter the main breach at the Kashmir Bastion; Column No. 2 was to storm the breach near the Water Bastion; Column No. 3, preceded by a forlorn hope (advance party) which was to plant an explosive charge and blow in the Kashmir Gate, was to enter by that route and then penetrate deep into the city as far as the Jumma Musjid mosque. Once inside the walls, these columns would be directed as their respective commanders saw fit, though columns 1 and 2 were to proceed along the inside walls of the city and open the Kabul Gate to No. 4. Column. No. 5 would be held as a reserve, to be committed as needed.

On the eve of the assault many of the troops settled down to compose what for some would be their final letter home. Captain Charles Ewart of the 2nd Bengal Fusiliers explained to his mother what the task involved:

Blowing of the Kashmir Gate. One of the most remarkable events in the history of the Mutiny, Lieutenant Philip Salkeld of the Bengal Engineers, lying mortally wounded, passes the portfire meant to light the explosive charge to Lieutenant Duncan Home of the same unit. The bugler, Robert Hawthorne of the 52nd, prepares to sound the advance. (Philip Haythornthwaite)

I believe we are to escalade. You know what that will be – rush up a ladder with men trying to push you down, bayonet and shoot you from above. But you must wave your sword and think it capital fun, bring your men up as fast as you can and jump down on top of men ready with fixed bayonets to receive you. All this is not very pleasant to think coolly of, but when the moment comes excitement and the knowledge that your men are looking to you to lead them on and bring them up with a cheer makes you feel as happy as possible ... It will be fearfully exciting work.

At 3am on the 14th, the columns moved up to their appointed positions under the covering fire of the siege guns. Once the breaches were cleared of the new defences established by the rebels during the night, the signal for the attack was made, with ominous orders to take no prisoners. As the first two columns rushed forward the rebels issued a tremendous fire of musketry from the walls high above and hurled down blocks of masonry, causing severe casualties. But the attackers, many encumbered with scaling ladders, carried on undaunted. Captain Richard Barter of the 75th Highlanders recorded the attack:

We had been watching anxiously for it, and now in columns of fours we rushed at the double through a high archway into a garden of roses and through this to the foot of the glacis. The dark forms of the 60th Rifles seemed to spring out of the earth, keeping up a galling fire on the walls and breach ... Day had broken and the sun was showing like a large red ball in the east as, passing through the line of the 60th who cheered us loudly, we emerged on the glacis and there, straight before us, was the breach. It was a huge

BELOW Hodson's Horse in combat at Rohtak, near Delhi, 17 August 1857. Leading his own irregular cavalry unit of 230 Sikhs and Punjabi Muslims, plus 125 other horsemen, William Hodson defeats a rebel cavalry force threatening the Anglo-Indian position on the Ridge.

ABOVE The storming of Delhi. Despite suffering severe casualties during six days of bitter fighting, the Anglo-Indian army prevailed and broke the back of the Mutiny. (British Library)

gap in the wall, full of men whose heads showed just over the edges of it. Along the walls they swarmed as thick as bees, the sun shining full on the white turbans and the black faces, sparkling brightly on their swords and bayonets. Our men cheered madly as they rushed on. The enemy, whose fire had slackened when ours ceased, at first seemed perfectly taken aback by our sudden appearance, but recovering from their surprise they now began firing again in earnest. Round shot came screaming from the guns far on our right, while grape and shell whistled from those nearer, and the walls seemed one line of fire all along our front. Bullets whipped through the air and tore up the ground about our feet and men fell fast ... Three times the ladder parties were swept away, and three times the ladders were snatched from the shoulders of the dead and wounded.

It was by these means that columns 1 and 2 burst into the city.

Storming of the Kashmir Gate. The odds against recapture were always heavy, but the British sensibly refrained from a premature assault and patiently awaited the arrival of reinforcements. (Philip Haythornthwaite)

The task before Column No. 3 was rather different, for its forward party were responsible for blowing in the Kashmir Gate to allow access to the city. What followed has become enshrined as one of the great military epics of the Victorian era: a small party of Bengal Sappers and Miners led by lieutenants Duncan Home and Philip Salkeld rushed to the gate, with the intention of placing a 25lb (11kg) sack of gunpowder against the door, blowing it down and sounding the advance. The prospect of success was extemely slim, and, in the event, many of the 'explosion party' as it was known, were hit by enemy fire. But the bags were duly set in place, the portfire was applied to the fuses, and, in a shattering explosion of flying splinters and brickwork, the right-hand door of the gate was blown off its hinges. On hearing a bugler sound the advance, the column rushed in through the archway, overpowered those rebels still capable of resistance, and met up with the other two assault columns in the Main Guard, where the reserve column soon appeared.

Thereafter, the rebels bitterly contested progress through the city streets, the whole affair characterized by savage house-to-house fighting down narrow alleys, with fire directed on the attackers from rooftops and through loopholed walls. But those who entered Delhi, though heavily outnumbered, were fired with an unquenchable desire for revenge. They wanted more than the city itself: they wanted blood. Countless mutineers and civilians were killed by incandescent British troops. One observer noted:

All the city people found within the walls when our troops entered were bayoneted on the spot; and the number was considerable, as you may suppose, when I tell you that in some houses forty or fifty persons were hiding. These were not mutineers but residents of the city, who trusted to our well-known mild rule for pardon. I am glad to say they were disappointed.

Disaster nearly struck, however, when part of Column No. 4 was routed, and the triumphant rebels pushed through the Kabul

The 52nd Foot storming a breach in the walls of Delhi. Just prior to the attack, Brevet-Major Anson of the 9th Lancers wrote bitterly to his wife: 'We may soon ... drive these bloodthirsty, dastardly villains into the Tartarus from which they spring, or they shall send us to the Heaven we pray for.' (Philip Haythornthwaite)

and Lahore Gates to counter-attack the main body, forcing it back towards the Ridge. The situation appeared critical, but the artillery and cavalry defending the camp managed to hold the rebels back, and when No. 2 Column stormed the Mori Bastion and the Kabul Gate from within the city, the threat to the Ridge was averted.

Meanwhile, the savage fighting continued, and though No. 3 Column had reached the Jumma Musjid Mosque, without artillery or explosives to hand it was impossible to break through the bricked-up arches and sandbags, obliging the column to withdraw to St James's Church. Shortly thereafter Nicholson was mortally wounded while directing his column towards the Lahore Gate. Circumstances were grim: only a quarter of the city had been taken, the Field Force had suffered massive casualties – 1,700 killed and wounded, or about a quarter of the attacking force – Nicholson was incapacitated, and No. 4 Column had been defeated. There was every possibility, based upon the rate of casualties thus far sustained, that Wilson's force would literally fight itself out of existence. Withdrawal began to look like the best course of action.

Wilson's subordinates strongly advised otherwise, and on the morning of 16 September, the day after many men had indulged in a drunken orgy on discovering a large cache of wine abandoned by the city's merchants, the advance proceeded, the streets being cleared methodically, house by house. Several key points were found empty or lightly defended, which indicated that the rebels were losing heart. The magazine was stormed and taken with little resistance, and yielded up 171 pieces of ordnance and a large stock of ammunition. The fighting continued on the 17th, but by then Wilson's force was down to 3,000 exhausted, filthy men, some of whom could make no further progress. Eventually, on the 19th, they managed to storm the Burn Bastion, and on the following morning the Lahore Gate was captured, enabling troops to be dispatched to

The King's Palace, also known as the Red Fort, boasted walls 110ft (33.5m) high surrounded by a wide and deep ditch. It served both as the royal palace of the titular King of Delhi, Bahadur Shah, the last of the Mughal emperors, and as a citadel. (British Library)

take the Ajmir Gate and the Jumma Musjid Mosque, both of which fell with little difficulty. Finally, the gate of the palace, known as the Red Fort, was blown in, and the last fanatical supporters of the king killed off. This marked the end of effective resistance in the city. Those not killed or wounded escaped unmolested through the south of the city or across the Jumna.

Bakht Khan had fled the vicinity of Delhi entirely, but the king was known to have taken refuge in the tomb of the Emperor Hamayun, 6 miles (9.6km) from the city. Confronted on the 21st by Major William

Brigadier-General John Nicholson, a stern, deeply religious veteran of both Anglo-Sikh wars, who in July 1857 led his 'Moveable Column' of lightly armed and equipped cavalry corps from the Punjab to assist the siege operations against Delhi. His arrival on the Ridge in early August raised British morale considerably. (Philip Haythornthwaite)

Total casualties from enemy action during the whole period of the siege were about 1,000 killed and 2,800 wounded, slightly over half of whom were British. In addition to this, many British troops had died of dysentery, cholera, heat stroke and other afflictions. Nicholson died of his wound on the 23rd, aware that the city had been retaken. Delhi was plundered for several days; valuables worth many hundreds of thousands of pounds were ultimately sold off by the prize agents, with the proceeds distributed to the men, but undeclared loot probably exceeded even this.

Large numbers of sepoys fled the city to join their comrades still fighting in other parts of the country, while some British troops were now released for operations elsewhere in Oudh, including 2,700 men under Colonel Edward Greathed, who left Delhi on 24 September and reached the besieged fort at Agra on 10 October.

Hodson, commander of an irregular Indian cavalry regiment, and his troopers, the king surrendered and was led back to Delhi. On learning that the king's three sons were also in hiding, Hodson returned the following day; in rapid succession he shot dead all three of them, despite the presence of a large hostile crowd which, impressed by Hodson's apparent indifference to the danger, declined to intervene.

Operations in and around Cawnpore, June–July 1857

Cawnpore, a city of 60,000 inhabitants in Oudh, the most disaffected province in British India, stood on the important communications route up the Ganges from Calcutta. Any relief force bound for Lucknow would have to pass through it. The city's garrison was led by Major-General Sir Hugh Wheeler, who had spent almost 50 years in India, and had married an Indian woman. He spoke the language of his troops, whom he respected and in whose loyalty he had absolute and, it transpired, misplaced, faith. On 4 June the sepoy regiments of the garrison rose up and from the 6th laid siege to Wheeler's small British contingent, comprising only 300 British officers and men, many of whom were sick, plus a handful of loyal Indian troops. Wheeler's

Nana Sahib and his escort. An heir to the Maratha kingdom, but dispossessed and receiving a pension from the East India Company, Nana Sahib accepted the rebels' invitation to take command of their forces in and around Cawnpore. (Philip Haythornthwaite)

situation was considerably weakened by the encumbrance of 500 civilians, most of them women and children. Erroneously believing the city and barracks themselves to be indefensible, Wheeler moved his force and its dependants into a small entrenchment outside the city, about a mile (1.6km) from the Ganges. In doing so Wheeler defied the entreaties of most of his staff, who preferred holding out in the magazine, a substantial building, easily capable of being fortified, containing a large amount of weapons and powder, much of it unnecessarily abandoned to the mutineers.

The new position consisted of a few barrack huts surrounded by a low, unfinished earth rampart no more than 4ft (1.2m) high, feebly backed by a shallow trench on the inside perimeter. Wheeler's command and its dependants had woefully inadequate provisions, though they were well supplied with small arms – enough in any event to enable each soldier to have several loaded weapons at his disposal. On the other hand, the defenders possessed almost no artillery: just six light guns, none of them properly

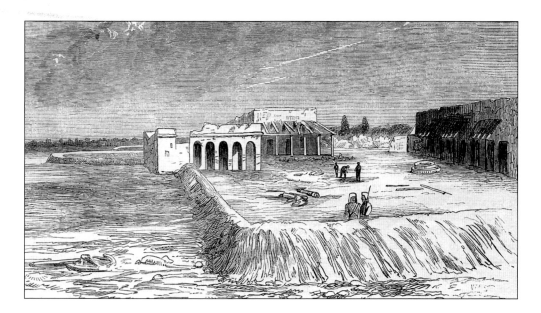

The entrenchment at Cawnpore. Major-General Wheeler's decision to establish his defences behind a rudimentary embankment in a 4-acre (1.6-hectare) unsheltered plain defied military logic and ultimately sealed the fate of the defenders; his subordinates had rightly advised him to hold out in the city's powerfully built arsenal. (Author's collection)

deployed. Wheeler's preference for this exceedingly weak position over that of the more obvious choice in the city centre remains a mystery today.

The rebels in and around Cawnpore, meanwhile, chose as their leader Dhondu Pant, known as the Nana Sahib, the Maharajah of Bithur and an heir of the Marathas, who had been dispossessed of most of their lands by the Company earlier in the century. Between 6 and 27 June the defenders endured terrible hardships before Wheeler, his ammunition, food and water nearly exhausted, recognized that further resistance was futile and surrendered in return for a promise of safe conduct down the Ganges to Allahabad.

The survivors of the three-week ordeal were duly escorted to the river bank where, as they began to board boats, they were treacherously fired upon by troops emerging from concealed positions on both banks. When musketry and cannon fire failed to account for all the men, sepoys waded into the water

and dispatched the rest with swords and bayonets. Numerous women and children also died, but the survivors were marched back into town, this time to the Bibigarh (House of the Ladies), a small bungalow once the residence of a British officer's mistress. The place consisted of two rooms, about 16ft^2 (4.9m^2), into which 206 women and children – the number representing the addition of other women and children captured elsewhere – were crammed.

Meanwhile, at Allahabad, a city on the Ganges just south of the border with Oudh, which contained a major arsenal, 62-year-old Brigadier-General Sir Henry Havelock was assembling a relief force for Lucknow, where a sizeable body of British troops and civilians, together with Indian allies and dependent non-combatants, were under siege in the British Residency. As Cawnpore lay on the road to Lucknow, relieving the former en route required no diversion: he would move north to Cawnpore, then cross the Ganges into Oudh and eastwards to Lucknow – an extremely difficult task for a force of about 2,000 men and six guns.

On 7 July Havelock began a gruelling 126-mile (203km) march in dreadful heat, aware that all the men of the Cawnpore garrison had been slaughtered and that the surviving women and children were being

Cawnpore

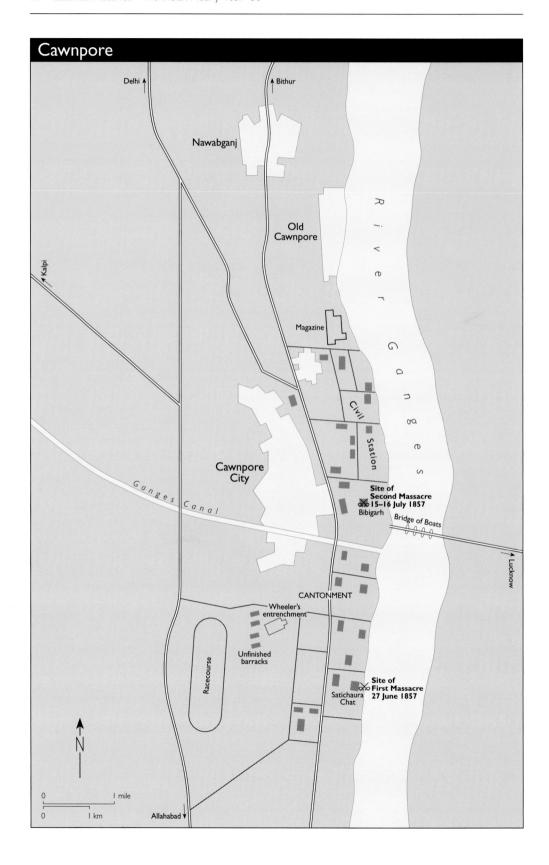

Delhi ↑

↑ Bithur

Nawabganj

Kalpi ↗

Old Cawnpore

R i v e r   G a n g e s

Magazine

Civil Station

Cawnpore City

Ganges Canal

Site of
Second Massacre
15–16 July 1857
Bibigarh   Bridge of Boats

↗ Lucknow

CANTONMENT

Wheeler's entrenchment

Racecourse

Unfinished barracks

Site of
First Massacre
27 June 1857
Satichaura Chat

N

0	1 mile
0	1 km

Allahabad ↓

Margaret Wheeler, the 18-year-old daughter of the British commander at Cawnpore. This heroic Victorian portrayal of her is in fact entirely fanciful – meant to provide a heroic tinge to the unspeakable truth: rescued from the first massacre at the river by a rebel sowar (cavalryman), she was forced to become a concubine, adopted native dress, and eventually settled in Cawnpore, apparently too ashamed to reveal her identity, which she only acknowledged on her deathbed, fifty years after the Mutiny, when she summoned a Catholic priest to administer the last rites. (Corbis)

held captive in the city. Progress was slow, for Havelock's men were not accustomed to long marches in such sweltering heat: temperatures often exceeded 100 degrees (37.7°C). Even when their heavy woollen jackets were placed in the baggage in favour of lighter dress, heatstroke exacted a heavy toll on the troops, many of them young recruits, unaccustomed to the rigorous conditions of service in India.

After a series of forced marches, largely conducted at night to avoid the worst of the heat, Havelock encountered 3,500 rebels with 12 guns at Fatehpur on 12 July. Underestimating Havelock's strength, the rebels attacked with great enthusiasm, only to find their determination checked when a British battery brought

down the rebel commander's elephant with the first shot. In the course of just 10 minutes the rebels were driven off, probably with negligible losses. In this, the first major encounter between the two sides in the field, Havelock emerged completely unscathed, though a dozen of his men collapsed and died from heatstroke.

After defeating the rebels again, at Aong, 10 miles (16km) closer to Cawnpore, where it turned their flank on 15 July, the relief force brushed aside another enemy contingent at Pandu Nadi later the same day. At last, Havelock faced Nana Sahib's main body of perhaps 10,000 men and eight guns outside Cawnpore itself, on the 16th. Havelock's artillery could not be brought into action owing to the exhausted state of the transport oxen in the ferocious heat, and he found his men exposed to heavy fire from the enemy's guns. 'I was resolved that this state of things could not last,' Havelock wrote in his dispatch,

... so calling upon my men, who were lying down in line, to leap to their feet, I directed another steady advance. It was irresistible! The enemy sent round shot into our ranks until we were within three hundred yards [274m], and

then poured in grape with such precision as I have seldom witnessed. But the 64th [Foot] … were not to be denied. Their rear showed the ground strewed with wounded; but on they steadily and silently came, then with a cheer charged and captured the unwieldy trophy of their valour [the rebel guns]. The enemy lost all heart, and after a hurried fire of musketry gave way in total rout. Four of my guns came up, and completed their discomfiture by a heavy cannonade.

The mutineers were broken up and Nana Sahib fled. Havelock's men, only a few miles from the city, lay down and slept outside the city, in anticipation of liberating the captives the following day. After marching 126 miles (203km) in eight days, and fighting four pitched battles against heavy odds, they simply could go no farther.

In fact, there were no prisoners to liberate. Probably angered by his failure to stem Havelock's advance, and determined not to give the British the satisfaction of recovering their compatriots, Nana Sahib had ordered the deaths of the prisoners. Accordingly, on the evening of 15–16 July, a handful of men, now believed to have been local butchers armed with swords and knives, entered the Bibigarh and hacked the helpless occupants to death. The carnage carried on through the night until, at about 8am the following day, three or four men were ordered to pitch the

LEFT Brigadier-General Sir Henry Havelock, one of several British commanders of the Mutiny who regarded the suppression of the revolt as his Christian duty. He recaptured Cawnpore before bringing reinforcements to Lucknow. (Author's collection)

BELOW The battle of Fatehpur, 12 July 1857. Brigadier-General Sir Henry Havelock, with about 1,400 British and 500 Indian troops, severely defeats a numerically superior rebel force during his march from Allahabad to Cawnpore. (Philip Haythornthwaite)

ABOVE Highlanders charging at Cawnpore, 15 July 1857. Troops advancing to the relief of the city endured terrible hardships and encountered rebel resistance on four separate occasions. (Philip Haythornthwaite)

dismembered bodies down a nearby dry well. A few survivors were thrown down alive, including several young children.

Just after dawn on the 17th, an advance party from Havelock's force entered the town and discovered the rebels had gone. Upon arriving at the Bibigahr they discovered to their horror the grisly evidence of the second massacre perpetrated at Cawnpore. One eyewitness recorded:

I never was more horrified! The place was one mass of blood. I am not exaggerating when I tell you that the soles of my boots were more than covered with the blood of these poor wretched creatures. [I found] quantities of dresses, clogged thickly with blood, children's frocks, frills, and ladies' under clothing of all kinds, also boys' trousers, leaves of Bibles … and hair, nearly a yard long; bonnets all bloody, and one or two shoes … All the way to the well was marked by a regular track along which the bodies had been dragged, and the thorny bushes had entangled in them scraps of clothing and long hairs. I have looked upon death in every form, but I could not look down that well again.

Havelock ordered the well, 50ft (15m) deep with human remains piled to within 6ft (1.8m) of the top, filled in with earth and sealed.

Brigadier-General James Neill, one of Havelock's subordinates, determined to exact a dreadful form of retribution for the massacre:

Wherever a rebel is caught he is immediately tried; and, unless he can prove a defence, he is sentenced to be hanged at once: the chief rebels, or ringleaders, I make first clean up a certain portion of the pool of blood, still two inches deep, in the shed where the fearful murder and mutilation of women and children took place. To touch blood is most abhorrent to the high-caste natives; they think, by doing so, they doom their souls to perdition. Let them think so. My object is to inflict a fearful punishment for a revolting, cowardly, barbarous deed, and to strike terror into these rebels... No one who has witnessed the scenes of murder, mutilation, and massacre, can ever listen to the word 'mercy', as applied to these fiends.

News of the massacre at Cawnpore had an equally powerful effect on British public opinion back home. Having tried to

The first massacre at Cawnpore, 27 June 1857. This atrocity, together with a second one committed three weeks later, not only contributed to the vengeful spirit which henceforth permeated the ranks of British forces in India, but inflamed the press and public back home. (National Army Museum)

introduce 'civilization' and Christianity to a 'heathen' race, the British had discovered such blessings were not merely rejected, but violently so. From pulpits across the country preachers began to speak of revenge rather than redemption. A total of 25,000 people assembled in the Crystal Palace to hear the enraged Baptist minister, Charles Spurgeon, demand retribution on a scale which would far exceed that committed by the rebels:

My friends, what crimes they have committed! ... The [British] Indian government [in Calcutta] never ought to have tolerated the religion of the Hindoos at all. If my religion consisted of bestiality, infanticide and murder, I should have no right to it unless I was prepared to be hanged. The religion of the Hindoos is no more than a mass of the rankest filth that imagination ever conceived. The Gods they worship are not entitled to the least atom of respect. Their worship necessitates everything that is evil and morality must put it down. The sword must be taken out of its sheath, to cut off our fellow subjects by their thousands.

The mutineers, in short, were to reap the whirlwind, and after Cawnpore the corpses of mutineers and suspected mutineers dangling from trees marked the route of advancing British columns whose commanders simply dispensed with the ordinary course of justice and applied their own summary form. According to Lieutenant Kendal Coghill, 'We burnt every village and hanged all the villagers who had treated our fugitives badly until every tree was covered with scoundrels hanging from every branch.' William Forbes-Mitchell of the 93rd, remarking on the barbarity of the conflict, described it as 'a *guerre à la mort* – a war of the most cruel and exterminating form,

in which no quarter was given on either side ... It was a war of downright butchery.' *The Times* reflected the feverish desire for retribution which animated a large proportion of its readership when it demanded that 'every tree and gable-end in the place should have its burden in the shape of a mutineer's carcass'.

Havelock left Neill and a small force at Cawnpore, and proceeded as quickly as he could towards Lucknow, which he was anxious to reach before the tragedy at Cawnpore could be repeated there.

The siege of Lucknow, June–November 1857

Meanwhile, dramatic events were unfolding at Lucknow, the capital of the province of Oudh, and seat of the British Resident. Lucknow possessed no military importance for either the British or the rebels, but it represented a thorn in the side of those who wished to re-establish the independent principality of Oudh on the one hand, and symbolized British defiance on the other. In Lucknow, Brigadier-General Sir Henry Lawrence, Chief Commissioner for the province and elder brother of Sir John Lawrence, Chief Commissioner of the Punjab, found himself in the midst of a hostile force, for Oudh stood at the very heart of the rebellion. Having lived in India for most of his life and having himself served in the Bengal Army, he was aware of the disaffection amongst the native troops and had taken steps to defend the garrison and its families in the event of a mutiny. His force numbered 1,720 men, about 700 of whom were Indian troops, plus 153 civilian

volunteers, and 1,280 non-combatants.
The mutineers, on the other hand,
numbered between 50,000 and
100,000 in and around the city.

Lucknow, a jumbled, maze-like city, with
walled gardens criss-crossing everywhere,
palaces, temples, mosques and residences,
extended in a great sprawl with the river
Gumtee to the east and a canal to the
south. On the northern end of the city lay
the British Residency, surrounded by walls
and sitting on a plateau. Apart from on its
northern side, the Residency was surrounded
by buildings which stood up against its
walls, and in some places overlooked
them. As early as May, Lawrence had
begun to fortify his position, establishing a
perimeter manned with troops and artillery,
and occupying a dilapidated fort known as
the Muchhee Bhowan about half a mile
(0.8km) to the north. He also gathered food,
ammunition and fodder. In the event of an
uprising, Lawrence planned to evacuate
the European portion of the city into the
Residency, for only one British regiment,
the 32nd Foot, was stationed in the city.

Lawrence received news of the mutiny at
Meerut on 14 May, whereupon he disbanded
a local sepoy irregular unit. He also learned
that sepoy units within his own garrison,
including one cavalry regiment, three
infantry regiments and a battery of artillery,
were thought to be planning to mutiny on
the night of the 30th. This information was
correct. Before the mutineers could inflict
any damage they were driven from the city
by the 32nd Foot and a battery of Bengal
Artillery, with an all-British crew. That day
the city's European population was assembled
in the Residency. Part of the 32nd remained
in the north of the city to observe the rebel
lines; the rest were stationed in the area of
the Residency, which was fortified, its walls
strengthened, windows blocked up, and
stocked with provisions and ammunition.

By mid-June Lawrence was aware that all
the British outposts in Oudh had been taken
by the rebels and that he faced the enemy
alone, with no aid immediately to hand.
Before the month was out news arrived

of the fall of Cawnpore and the surrender
of its garrison, though its fate was not yet
known. Oddly enough, the mutineers made
no attempt to harass the British garrison
at Lucknow until 29 June, when a body of
troops estimated at 500 infantry, 50 cavalry
and one gun was thought to have arrived at
Chinhut, 10 miles (16km) away. In reality,
the mutineers numbered over ten times that
number. Lawrence neglected to send out a
reconnoitring party to determine the strength
or exact position of the enemy before
foolishly leading a force to confront it on
the 30th, when he left the city with 300 men
from the 32nd Foot, 170 loyal sepoys, about

100 cavalry and 11 guns. Trained and dressed virtually identically to Lawrence's troops, the mutineers inflicted 200 casualties and took five guns before forcing him back into the Residency to lick his wounds. Writing to Havelock, Lawrence warned: 'The enemy has followed us up, and ... unless we are relieved quickly, say in fifteen or twenty days, we shall hardly be able to maintain our position.'

Now realizing the strength of the force opposing him, Lawrence ordered the men in the Muchhee Bhowan to withdraw from their position under cover of darkness and blow it up. Lieutenant-Colonel John Inglis of the 32nd, the second-in-command,

writing to Calcutta with a report on the situation, identified the chief danger as well as his disappointment with Lawrence's handling of the defence:

Our heaviest losses have been caused by fire from the enemy's sharpshooters, stationed in the adjoining mosques and houses of the native nobility, the necessity of destroying which

The Bibigarh, site of the second massacre at Cawnpore, after its discovery by Havelock's troops. The most infamous atrocity of the Mutiny, the wholesale murder of women and children here, enflamed British sensibilities and contributed to the merciless spirit of vengeance which marked the fighting thereafter. (Author's collection)

had been repeatedly drawn to the attention of Sir Henry [Lawrence] by the staff of engineers … As soon as the enemy had thoroughly completed the investment of the Residency they occupied these houses, some of which were within easy pistol shot of our barricades, in immense force, and rapidly made loopholes on those sides which bore on our post, from which they kept up a terrific and incessant fire, day and night, which caused us many daily casualties… Moreover, there was no place in the whole of our works that could be considered safe, for several of the sick and wounded, lying in the banqueting hall, which had been turned into a hospital, were killed in the very centre of the building.

Lawrence himself did not survive for long: on 2 July he was mortally wounded in his room by an exploding shell, and he died two days later. Command devolved upon Inglis, who received a promotion to brigadier-general. Inglis took immediate action, launching a series of sorties against the mutineers' forward posts and spiking their guns, thus raising the garrison's battered morale and steeling it against the occasional attacks and regular sniping. The siege settled into a wearisome contest punctuated by intermittent artillery

The infamous 'Well of the Innocents' at Cawnpore. Having butchered their captives on the night of 15–16 July 1857, Nana Sahib's men flung the dismembered bodies down this dry well, where the gruesome remains were discovered by the horrified men of Havelock's relief force. (Author's collection)

bombardments, the regular rattle of musket fire, and constant sniping. On some days the mutineers would launch concerted attacks against the defenders, but all such forays were driven back, sometimes with heavy losses. The outposts were obliged to remain ever-vigilant for fear of being overrun. A captain of the 25th Native Infantry, having fortified his house, described what would befall the whole of the garrison in the event of defeat:

We well knew what we had to expect if we were defeated, and therefore each individual fought for his very life. Each loophole displayed a steady flash of musketry, as defeat would have been certain death to every soul in the garrison... During this time even the poor wounded men ran out of the hospital, and those who had wounds in their legs threw away their crutches and deliberately knelt down and fired as fast as they could; others, who could do little else, loaded the muskets.

In time, as musketry was shown to be relatively ineffective against the British defences, the rebels adopted the practice of mining. Inglis's engineers dug counter-mines and fought bitterly in the tunnels beneath the Residency walls, generally gaining the upper hand over the attackers. Nevertheless, on 10 August, the rebels managed to detonate a mine which destroyed 20ft (18m) of the defences and part of a house, in so doing creating a large enough breach to invite attack. The explosion may have been premature, for the handful of mutineers who actually made for the gap were shot down or driven off by a devastating fire directed from the rooftop of the mess-house.

The mutineers were only one of the dangers facing those besieged in the Residency. A quieter, but equally deadly, enemy operated from within. Overcrowding and poor sanitation made an excellent breeding ground for diseases such as cholera, dysentery and small-pox, all exacerbated by the virtual impossibility of disposing of the dead. The women behaved with extreme patience and at times valour, undertaking nursing duties, improvising uniforms for

The British Residency at Hyderabad, in the Deccan, one of the many regions in India which remained loyal to the Raj. The local ruler, the nizam, deployed artillery to disperse a Muslim mob that attacked this complex in July 1857. (Author's collection)

soldiers, keeping ration records and lists of casualties, collecting firewood, and bringing tea and alcohol to the men manning the defences. By the end of the siege, as many people had died of, or were incapacitated by, disease as by enemy fire. A chronic shortage of food, which resulted in scurvy and other diseases, compounded other problems, such as heatstroke, trauma, rashes, boils and nervous strain, all of which exacted a daily toll. Doctors were scarce, though it is of note that amongst the garrison was Dr William Brydon, who had reached Jellalabad as one of the last survivors of the army that had left Kabul on its disastrous retreat in 1842 during the Afgan war. Without adequate space for care of the wounded and sick, those without beds lay in rows on the floor, surrounded by flies and the dreadful stench of gangrene and decomposition. Still, those who could stand and fight did so when the alarm was sounded; the less fit loaded weapons if they had the strength to do so. All were acutely aware that their lives depended on a successful defence, for the fall of the Residency would result in wholesale massacre.

For the whole of August and into September circumstances remained largely unchanged: no prospect of relief for the garrison, with the enemy continuing to snipe, mine and bombard the Residency while its occupants dwindled through enemy action and disease.

ABOVE Brigadier-General Sir Henry Lawrence, Chief Commissioner of Oudh. Although he committed a few notable blunders, with proper intelligence and foresight, Lawrence took practical steps to defend Lucknow in the event of mutiny, saved the lives of hundreds of civilians by evacuating them in time to the Residency, and occupied the attention of thousands of mutineers who might otherwise have moved on Delhi. (Philip Haythornthwaite)

The reliefs of Lucknow

Both the British government and public were aware of the heroic resistance maintained by the defenders of the Residency, and although Lucknow was of no military importance, the spirit of defiance it came to symbolize ensured that a serious effort would be made to relieve it.

It will be recalled that Havelock had been dispatched from Allahabad in early July to relieve Lucknow, in the course of which march he retook Cawnpore on the 17th of that month. Determined to press on to rescue the defenders of the Residency, he resumed his march on the 25th, when he bridged the Ganges, and entered Oudh. The rebels unsuccessfully confronted him several times near Unao, and by mid-August cholera, casualties and the heat had reduced his command to a mere 1,500 men and ten guns, for which his supply of ammunition had become nearly exhausted. With a large rebel army based at Bithur threatening his flank, Havelock realized that he must retire to Cawnpore and await reinforcements. The

two sides met outside Bithur on 16 August, when Havelock drove Nana Sahib's force of about 4,000 men through the town and into the stream behind, after which he burned Nana Sahib's palace.

By 15 September, substantial numbers of reinforcements under Major-General Sir James Outram had arrived at Cawnpore, increasing Havelock's relief force to over 3,000 men (2,000 of these being British infantry). Outram outranked Havelock and ought to have superseded him, but he graciously waived his seniority so that Havelock would receive credit for the relief of Lucknow. Outram thereafter accompanied the army in his civil capacity as Chief Commissioner of Oudh, to resume command once the city was retaken. Havelock crossed the Ganges on 19 September and fought a minor, though successful, action at Mangalwar three days later. The bridge spanning the river Sai was discovered intact and on the 22nd the relief column reached

LEFT Attack on the Redan Battery at Lucknow. Though they fought with courage and tenacity, the mutineers lacked proper leadership and could not equal their opponents man for man. The regimental organization of sepoy units gradually disintegrated, reducing their fighting effectiveness. Thrown together, the rebels found themselves unable to manoeuvre with the same efficiency as before. Discipline and morale naturally suffered as a result, exacerbated by disagreements over command and pay. (Philip Haythornthwaite)

ABOVE Defenders of Lucknow on watch. Subject to relentless sniper fire, intermittent attacks and the entirely unseen threat of mines, the soldiers and civilians besieged in the Residency held out unassisted for three months. (Philip Haythornthwaite)

Bani, only 16 miles (26km) from Lucknow – close enough to hear the sound of the enemy's guns bombarding the Residency.

On the morning of the 23rd Havelock resumed his march, encountering approximately 11,500 rebels with a good complement of artillery about 4 miles (nearly 6.5km) south of Lucknow. A marsh protected part of their line, while their left stood anchored on the Alambagh, a group of walled buildings and enclosed gardens 2 miles (just over 3km) outside the city. Havelock's artillery drove off the rebel cavalry and silenced their guns, whereupon their infantry broke and ran. Those who attempted to defend the Alambagh were driven out at the point of the bayonet.

On the same day Havelock and Outram received news of the fall of Delhi, greatly boosting the column's morale. The two commanders now had to develop a plan for reaching the Residency, which was situated on the far side of the city. Their chosen route was intended to avoid, as far as possible, the narrow loopholed buildings of Lucknow's labyrinthine streets. First, they would seize the Char bridge, then move east with the canal on their right until they reached the palace along the river, and then proceed towards the Residency through a series of parks. In the event that he was repulsed, Havelock would pull back to the Alambagh, where he would leave a garrison of several hundred men, together with the sick and wounded, and the baggage.

The column began its advance on the morning of 25 September, encountering stiff opposition almost from the start, but it gradually cleared the enemy, many of whom stood behind the cover of walls and enclosures. Havelock's men seized the bridge, bayoneted the gunners defending it, and proceeded into a built-up area of temples, mosques, palaces, houses and gardens, from the protection of which the rebels offered stiff resistance. In many places the attackers used artillery to blast their way down the narrow lanes, accompanied where necessary by bayonet charges delivered with shouts of 'Remember Cawnpore!' Elements of the column stormed and took the Kaisarbagh (King's Palace), followed by the Chattur

LEFT Brigadier-General John Inglis, who, on the death of the indefatigable Sir Henry Lawrence in early July 1857, succeeded in command of the troops besieged in the Residency at Lucknow. (Philip Haythornthwaite)

BELOW The embattled British Residency at Lucknow. The bullet-riddled edifice that still remains has become a memorial to those who died defending it as well as to the civilians, two-thirds of whom perished from wounds, disease and exhaustion during the siege. Lucknow itself was not finally cleared of rebels until 21 March 1858, nine months after the siege had begun. (British Library)

Siege and reliefs of Lucknow

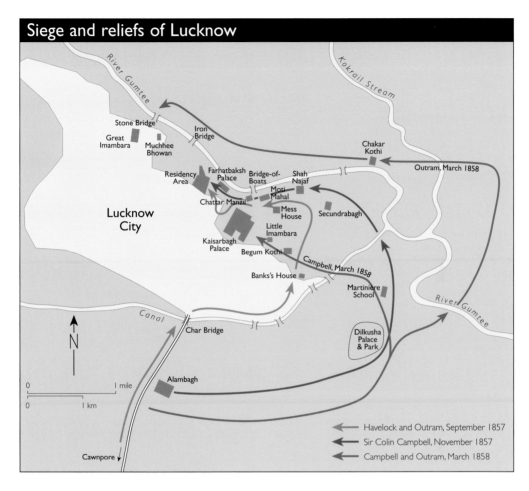

River Gumtee

Kokrail Stream

Stone Bridge

Great Imambara

Muchhee Bhowan

Iron Bridge

Chakar Kothi

Outram, March 1858

Residency Area

Farhatbaksh Palace

Bridge-of-Boats

Shah Najaf

Lucknow City

Chattar Manzil

Moti Mahal

Mess House

Secundrabagh

Little Imambara

Kaisarbagh Palace

Begum Kothi

Campbell, March 1858

Banks's House

Martinière School

River Gumtee

Canal

Char Bridge

Dilkusha Palace & Park

N

0   1 mile

0   1 km

Alambagh

Cawnpore

← Havelock and Outram, September 1857

← Sir Colin Campbell, November 1857

← Campbell and Outram, March 1858

Manzil (Old Palace). Then, with only 500 yards (457m) separating them from the gates of the Residency, Havelock's men encountered a street crossed by trenches and lined with loopholed houses on either side. The column had no choice but to run this terrible gauntlet, taking fearful casualties, including the merciless Neill, before reaching the Residency to the unrestrained joy and cheers of its embattled survivors. The price of relieving the place had been high: 535 killed or wounded.

Weakened by such severe casualties, together with losses sustained through disease, the 'relief' force was now only strong enough to reinforce and secure the Residency and occupy an enlarged area around it – including the Alambagh, physically separated but well-fortified – but could neither fight its way out nor evacuate the occupants to

Cawnpore. The mutineers therefore re-imposed the siege, which would continue for another six weeks, with Outram, now assuming command, revealing his knowledge of a secret cache of foodstuffs hidden beneath the Residency which Lawrence had stockpiled there without, unaccountably, informing the commissariat. By this good fortune, the newly enlarged garrison could be supplied for at least two more months, though it only highlighted the fact that, with the relieving force now itself besieged, further troops would be required to rescue them. The pursuit of the rebels elsewhere would have to wait.

A second relief column, under Brigadier-General Hope Grant, reached Cawnpore at the end of October and awaited reinforcements from General Sir Colin Campbell, the newly appointed commander-in-chief. After reorganizing the

the evacuation of the Residency, he then attacked the next formidable enemy strongpoint, the Secundrabagh, an enclosure about 120 yards square (110m²), built of strong masonry and loopholed on all sides, on the 16th. After 18-pdrs, firing at extremely close range, created a breach in the side of the building, the 93rd Highlanders were unleashed in reply to Campbell's exhortation, 'Bring on the tartan!' Wielding broadsword and bayonet, the men of the 93rd fought their way through successive rooms, working their way to the gate, which they opened to allow access for their comrades. The terrible slaughter in the confines of the Secundrabagh accounted for at least 2,000 rebels, plus 22 Highlanders killed and 75 wounded.

Gradually the column advanced, pounding its way through the streets with blasts of heavy artillery, peppering the enemy with musketry, and surging forward with the bayonet, in some places leaving mounds of dead and wounded in its wake. Against the next strongpoint, the Shah Najaf mosque,

ABOVE Sir Colin Campbell, the redoubtable, fiery and well-respected veteran of the Peninsular War, the Opium War, the Second Sikh War and the Crimean War, in the last of which he commanded the Highland Brigade. After taking command of the army in India, he relieved Lucknow and played an important role in the campaign of 1858. (Author's collection)

administration and transport, Campbell left Cawnpore for Lucknow in early November with 4,500 fresh troops, including a Naval Brigade of 250 sailors and marines from HMS *Shannon*, plus naval 24-pdrs that could blast through walls with roundshot or clear streets when loaded with grapeshot. Campbell reached the Alambagh on 12 November, adding its garrison to his own force, which now totalled 5,000 men and 49 guns. Then, on the 14th, on the basis of advice sent from the Residency by a courier in disguise, Campbell decided to take a different route from Havelock's.

First he drove the rebels from the Dilkusha Park with artillery fire, then he took the Martinère school. After bringing up supplies and wagons on the 15th in preparation for

only 500 yards (457m) to the north-west of the Secundrabagh, Campbell ordered an assault. Captain Peel, commanding the naval guns, battered away at the structure, behaving, Campbell wrote admiringly in his dispatch, 'very much as if he had been laying the *Shannon* alongside an enemy's frigate'. Nevertheless, the walls could not be breached, and by dawn the enemy had escaped through a gate at the rear. Campbell's force was now just 400 yards (366m) from the Residency, whose garrison could make out the regimental colours of the 93rd flying from the minaret of the Shah Najaf mosque.

On the following morning, the 17th, the last two main obstacles to the advance – the Mess House and the Moti Mahal, both fortified and loopholed – fell before Campbell's onslaught: the former taken in the first attempt, the second after the enemy resisted for an hour. At last Campbell broke through to Outram and Havelock in the Residency, and, beginning on the 19th, began evacuating the garrison and the civilians, including a large number of sick and wounded, plus an enormous quantity of treasure and the King of Oudh's jewels. The evacuation was carried out masterfully, and the enemy did not interfere in the process, which was completed on the 23rd. Havelock, worn out by fatigue and weakened by dysentery, died on the 24th. Outram remained behind to hold the Alambagh with 4,000 men and 35 guns.

Meanwhile, on the 27th, Campbell began the 40-mile (64km) march to Cawnpore, where the garrison of 1,000 men left behind under Major-General Windham had been defeated by 14,000 rebels with 40 guns under Tantia Topi. Thoroughly drubbing the mutineers on 6 December, Campbell took

BELOW Meeting of generals Havelock, Outram and Campbell during the second relief of Lucknow, 17 November 1857, after the Residency had undergone a siege of four and a half months. The garrison had been reinforced on 25 September when Havelock and Outram had fought their way in, but the siege was resumed until the arrival six weeks later of a more substantial army under Campbell. British and loyal Indian troops did not recover the city itself until March 1858. (National Army Museum)

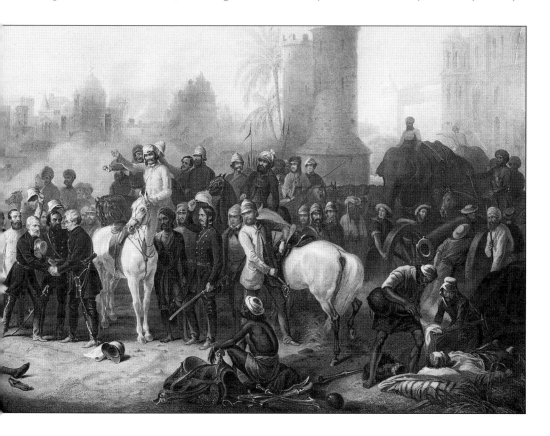

ABOVE The relief of Lucknow. While at first the women trapped in the Residency at Lucknow failed to cope without their husbands and servants, in time they rose to the task, helping in the kitchens and hospitals, loading weapons and performing other vital tasks, thus allowing the men to manage the defence of the place. (Philip Haythornthwaite)

16 guns, a massive quantity of stores, vehicles, ammunition and pack animals, before re-occupying the city, the civilians and wounded already having been dispatched on the 3rd to the safety of Allahabad.

Hereafter, notwithstanding the arrival of substantial reinforcements from abroad, Campbell conducted the campaign at a slower pace, securing communications with Delhi and the Punjab before moving again on Lucknow, though now with reinforcements from Nepal. Now it was the turn of the Anglo-Indians, now 20,000-strong, including 9,000 Gurkhas, to lay siege to Lucknow, beginning on 2 March 1858, with Outram's small force still in possession of the Alambagh. The number of defenders is not precisely known, but was estimated at approximately 120,000 (excluding civilians). Important points in the city fell in stages: the Martinière was taken on 9 March, the Begum Kothi (a fortified position) two days later, and on the 16th the Residency was captured.

By the 21st the city was back in British hands, though at a cost of 1,200 casualties and an untold, though certainly higher, cost to the mutineers. Campbell continued

operations against scattered rebel forces, though in general Anglo-Indian forces could not keep pace with their more mobile enemies and many rebels had escaped from Oudh to the neighbouring areas of Rohilkhand and Bihar, in central India. Defeating the mutineers fell to General Sir Hugh Rose.

The 93rd Highlanders at Lucknow. In full costume, including feather bonnets, plumes and kilts, Sir Colin Campbell's favourites fight their war into the Secundrabagh during the second relief of Lucknow in November 1857. Prior to battle Campbell told his men: 'When we make an attack you must come to close quarters as quickly as possible. Keep well together and use the bayonet ...You are my lads. I rely on you to do the work! (National Army Museum)

Brevet-Major O.H.S.G. Anson, 9th Lancers

At the beginning of the Mutiny, Brevet-Major Anson commanded a squadron of the 9th Lancers, one of the few mounted regiments of the British Army in India, and at various points during the conflict he commanded the regiment as a whole. By 1857 he had already served in India for nearly 20 years, and had fought at Punniar and Sobraon in the First Sikh War, and at Gujerat and Chilianwallah in the Second. His term of service in the Mutiny was in fact short, for though he took part in the siege and recapture of Delhi, his health seriously declined in March 1858, and he died the following January. In the course of his service on and around the Ridge at Delhi Anson frequently wrote to his wife, who, with many other civilians, had taken refuge at Kussowlee, a hill station much like Simla.

In early June the Delhi Field Force approached the city, passing through country dotted with old buildings, woods, swamps, dry canals and walled villages, which, in combination with the enemy's determined resistance, held up the column's advance. Finally reaching the Ridge, Anson's regiment took up a position near Hindu Rao's house, a derelict mansion of substantial strength. It soon became clear that the space in front of the Ridge had to be cleared of the enemy's skirmishers, for the Anglo-Indian force continued to come under fire from mutineers who used the extensive cover for sniping. Only 1,000 yards (914m) separated the batteries on the Ridge from the ramparts of Delhi, whose towering walls and bastions even Anson recognized as too formidable to breach with the calibre of guns available. He appreciated, too, that time was not on the side of the British, for cholera and other diseases took a constant toll on their numbers.

He often stood to watch British guns fire at the city, as 24lb (10.8kg) shot was returned. It was commonplace for both sides to re-fire spent shot at one another. On 12 June he noted how 'the big guns and mortars were firing fiercely all night on the enemy, who were very slack in returning the fire, and every minute our mortars or 24-pounders are sending them a pill; but we are too far off, and Delhi will never be taken in this way'. At times the enemy's fire was so heavy that Anson had to 'watch and dodge the cannon-balls'; apart from that, he found the heat and glare of the sun to be especially enervating. He made frequent reference in his letters to the many sorties made by the rebels, some of which harassed the picket of his regiment, which performed the vital task of protecting the flanks and rear of the camp.

Conditions on the Ridge were difficult, as Anson observed, but there was no chronic shortage of provisions. He complained of 'no good brandy' and noted the great expense of luxuries, such as tea, an 'extravagant treat', as well as sugar and beer, but there was soup, meat and onions – though no potatoes – as well as bread and butter 'washed down with sherry and water'. On another occasion he writes of 'goose, rice pudding and stewed guavas for dinner'.

In several respects Anson's attitudes reflected the popular opinion of his comrades on the Ridge, not least a complete confidence in ultimate success. Delhi would be re-taken: it was merely a matter of time. His correspondence moreover expressed a widespread confidence derived from faith. As he explained to his wife:

... it would be most cruel to think that God was not on our side. We have His own covenant and promise to guide and protect us eventually; but knowing India and our people in India as well as I do, I am not in the least surprised at His sending this severe judgment on us. I look

*upon the business in the light of a heavy
punishment for the ungodly, infidel lives
the greater part of us have lived in India.*

A few days later he added:

*Yes; the Lord may sacrifice us as a wicked
and adulterous generation, but there is nothing
more certain than that He is on our side, and
that after justly punishing us for our sins,
He will grind the heathen to powder.*

Through June and July the rebels
continued their attacks, particularly on
the camp's rear, where Anson was regularly
engaged. The rebels approached the Ridge
both during the day and night: 'I cannot
describe to you the confusion that ensued
in the dark, and how grand it was to see the
battle raging in the dark, when one could
see the flash of every matchlock.' Under
these circumstances, the troops were forced to
remain ever-vigilant, for no one could be sure
when the next sortie would come: 'we literally
know not what an hour may bring forth'.

The first rains arrived at the end of June,
which came in torrents, and while they
brought down the temperature – 'the air now
is delightfully cool and refreshing' – they
also made Anson feel 'out of sorts, heavy
about the head, sleepy, and lethargic'.
The rains carried on through July, and the
casualty lists grew. Anson's picquets, their
blue uniforms regularly drenched as they
made rounds of the camp, often came
under fire. When the sun re-appeared,
the temperature soared; Anson recorded
the temperature at 99 degrees (37.2°C) at
5.30pm one day. With the heat came clouds
of flies, obliging Anson 'to battle for every
mouthful'. Whenever men sat down to eat,
flying bugs of various descriptions descended
on the scene. There were scorpions, too, and
hundreds of camels 'blocking up the road
and frightening the horses. They are a
dreadful bother, all so scabby, diseased,
and stinking, too.'

Rebel sortie from Delhi. The mutineers launched
incessant attacks on the Ridge. Major Charles Reid
recorded 21 such forays in a single day, lasting from
7.30am until dark. 'Not a thing had we to eat,'
he complained, 'and we all came home dead beat.
I never felt so completely done up before. The sun was
something fearful.' (Anne S.K. Brown Military Collection)

The blowing of the Kashmir Gate, an exploit for which four Victoria Crosses were awarded, one posthumously. This epic of the Mutiny involved an 'explosion party' consisting of two British officers, three British NCOs, three Sikhs and a British bugler. (Anne S.K. Brown Military Collection)

The days passed wearily, with constant alarms at the approach of the enemy, bouts of heavy rain, thunder and lightning, followed by searing heat, and rising cases of cholera, heatstroke, dysentery and

the rebels continued to harass the camp from cover. 'There the enemy lie, snugly ensconced behind walls, nullah banks, and large stones, and plying you well at from 150 to 300 yards (37m to 274m) with their deadly small arms. We must advance to drive them away, and thus present them with very fair shots.' He described their method of attack thus:

They steal up in great numbers to within eighty or ninety yards [73m to 82m] of the picquet, and, firing off their muskets, run away as hard as they can, one of our batteries helping them to do so with a good grace. Our men being safe behind breastworks, their noisy volleys are perfectly innocuous.

During August Anson recorded several instances of the infantry being engaged for over 12 hours continuously, with a regular exchange of artillery fire. He spent many a sleepless night amidst the noise of the guns and shouts to the camp to repel an attack. The area below the Ridge had long since become pockmarked and scarred by artillery fire; trees had either been felled by the exchange of fire or cut down for firewood, until the landscape had become semi-desert. Over this scene of devastation, under a fierce sun, hung the repulsive stench of rotting animal carcasses and rebel corpses that Anson frequently encountered, in one instance 'an enormous mass of putrefaction in the form of a dead camel or bullock'.

Finally, on the morning of 14 August, to cheers from the entire camp, Nicholson's 'Moveable Column' appeared on the Ridge, with the band of the 52nd Foot playing, and two 24-pdrs and three 18-pdrs amongst the new arrivals. The siege train trundled into camp on 4 September, covering 13 miles (21km) of road, some of the heavier pieces of ordnance harnessed to elephants. In all, Anson counted six 24-pdrs, eight 18-pdrs, four 8-in howitzers, and four 10-in mortars – 22 pieces with hundreds of rounds of ammunition each. Armed with the right material for the job, Anson wrote to his wife:

exhaustion. 'Every day now,' he wrote on 20 July, 'some thirty or forty Europeans are expended by the enemy, the sun, disease, and fatigue; and as the season advances we may expect more sickness.' At the same time,

Assault on Delhi. Tactical wisdom dictates that an attacker should outnumber the defender by at least three to one. The fact that the Delhi Field Force stormed the city while itself heavily outnumbered bears testament to the bravery, determination and fighting skills of the besiegers. (Anne S.K. Brown Military Collection)

large working parties are now very busy preparing the batteries and approaches and in three days from this, if not sooner, there will be a flame of devouring fire and a tempest of shot all about the place. Two or three

days after the fire has once opened we shall,
like a flood of mighty waters overflowing,
storm the walls, and I fervently hope and
pray [that we] destroy these murderers
and burn up their city.

The men, ragged and exhausted, often
worked at night in preparing the batteries,
for during the day the temperature exceeded
90 degrees (32.2°C) under cloudless skies.
By 8 September several batteries, situated
between 600 and 700 yards (549m and 640m)
from the wall, began firing. In his general
orders to the troops, Anson records Major-
General Wilson's confidence

that British pluck and determination will
carry everything before them, and that the
bloodthirsty mutineers against whom they
are fighting will be driven headlong out of
their stronghold and be exterminated. But to
enable them to do this he warns the troops of
the absolute necessity of their keeping together
and not straggling from their columns; by this
only can success be secured. Major-General
Wilson need hardly remind the troops of the
cruel murders committed on their officers and
comrades, as well as their wives and children, to
move them in their deadly struggle. No quarter
should be given to the mutineers; at the same
time, for the sake of humanity and the honour
of the country they belong to, he calls upon
them to spare all women and children that
may come in their way.

Oxen gradually brought the heaviest
batteries forward, where, with the assistance
of many of the 9th Lancers, they began to
batter at the walls until a breach was made.
During the assault, the Ridge was to be held
by the sick and wounded, a few guns, and
the small body of available cavalry, including
Anson and various irregular units, who were
to hold the right to prevent any enemy
sorties emerging from the Lahore Gate
and threatening Wilson's now precariously
weakened position on the Ridge. When the
assault came, Anson's cavalry followed up
the infantry and stood outside the walls
amidst heavy fire from infantry high above.
When the rebels forced No. 4 Column back
out of the city and threatened the Ridge, the
9th Lancers and the Bengal Horse Artillery
kept the attackers in check, a process
which cost Anson's regiment a quarter
of its strength and 61 horses.

Amy Horne and the massacre at Cawnpore

Neither side during the Mutiny conducted itself with much honour. The rebels' wholesale massacre of European civilians had no moral basis, while the British spirit of revenge was more than primitive: it was atavistic. Both sides committed the most appalling atrocities in a conflict which marked the first occasion in which British women found themselves caught up in fighting on a large scale. As we have seen, the most horrifying and infamous of all the massacres perpetrated by the mutineers took place on two occasions – 27 June and 15 July 1857 – during the three-week siege of Cawnpore. Understandably, very few first-hand accounts of the two massacres at Cawnpore exist, perhaps the most remarkable from the first being left by Amy Horne, the 18-year-old step-daughter of a postal worker and the eldest child in a family with three other daughters and two sons, ranging in age from infancy to ten years.

Before the Mutiny, Cawnpore was considered an attractive British post, with a club, race-course and assembly rooms for balls and dances. The tranquillity of this fairly prosperous commercial city was broken on 14 May 1857 by the shocking news that mutiny had broken out at Meerut four days earlier. Notwithstanding the fact that the local Indian garrison outnumbered his British troops by ten to one, Major-General Sir Hugh Wheeler, the commander at Cawnpore, was not especially concerned. While the residents grew increasingly restless and the atmosphere more volatile, Wheeler chose not to incite panic by sending the women and children down river to the safety of Calcutta. When, however, news arrived on the morning of 31 May that mutiny had broken out at Lucknow, he ordered his small garrison and the city's Europeans into a hastily built entrenchment and the few buildings adjacent, provisioned this woefully inadequate position

for a month, and settled down to await relief. The sepoys in Cawnpore, recognizing the obvious weakness of Wheeler's position, immediately set fire to and sacked the British cantonments, after which, on 6 June, they laid siege to the entrenchment itself, whose buildings were not even extensive enough to protect its occupants from the intense sun.

The vulnerability of the entrenchment soon became clear, for the mutineers quickly mounted siege guns and, by midday on the 7th, what Horne described as 'our Lilliputian defences' became the target of an intense bombardment. Rebels occupied the surrounding buildings, between 300 and 800 yards (274m and 731m) away, and all day

a shower of bullets poured down upon us in our exposed position. Shells likewise kept falling all over ... One shell killed seven women as it fell hissing into the trenches and burst. Windows and doors were soon shot off their sockets, and the shot and ball began to play freely through the denuded buildings ...

The agonies we endured during the siege are indescribable. The men were in the trenches, under the burning rays of a June sun ... where the temperature in the shade is as high as 110 to 115 degrees Fahrenheit [43.3–46.1ºC]. It was not the heat alone that caused us intense suffering, but also the lack of food, water, and rest.

The garrison, Horne found, did the best that it could to provide for so many mouths to feed. Only a single well supplied fresh water for the defenders, and anyone attempting to draw from it attracted the particular attention of the rebels' artillery. Even when water was forthcoming, it could only be drunk as sips, for there was no knowing how long the garrison would have to hold out. Washing, of course, constituted a luxury no one could afford. As for food, Horne continued:

*Our troubles hourly increased, and we began
to feel the pangs of hunger, our provision-room
having shared the same fate as the other parts
of the building. My poor little brothers and
sisters, wee little things as they were, felt the
want of food dreadfully ... Infants were starved
to death on the maternal breasts, which famine
had dried of their nourishment.*

The last meal of any substance consisted
of horsemeat as the basis of a meagre soup.
Thereafter the occupants were reduced to
eating horse fodder once a day, with a
small quantity of rum. Many actually went
mad owing to the combined stresses of heat,
exhaustion, hunger and incessant musket and
artillery fire. Horne's mother was one of those
driven insane by the appalling conditions:

*I used to sit and listen to her ravings,
muttered in broken sentences. Her one theme
was her mother whom she wanted to see. At one
moment she would be calling for a conveyance
to take her to her mother, and the next her mind
would wander away to something else. Her
dreadful affliction rendered me heartbroken ...*

Conditions degenerated even further
when a shell set fire to the thatched roof of a
structure crowded with people. Panic ensued
and the women and children, fleeing from
the building, came under fire from shot
and shell. The soldiers, obliged to maintain
their positions in the trenches to repel
an expected rebel assault, could lend but
little assistance, and some of the sick and
wounded who could not be rescued died in
the flames or under the collapsing building.
Horne was herself wounded in the head,
and, like the other survivors, was obliged
to strip her dress of all unnecessary material
for the supply of bandages for the mounting
numbers of wounded.

The entrenchment had by now become a
hellish place, with children dying on a daily
basis, the supply of medicine exhausted, and
the intolerable combination of incessant
enemy fire, suffocating heat, flies and the
stench of unburied corpses wafting through
the entrenchment and the semi-demolished,

rat-infested buildings. The occupants remained
in this state for three weeks, the men defiantly
returning fire, yet the mutineers refusing to
assault the place. Finally, on 25 June, Nana
Sahib offered the promise of safe passage to
Allahabad provided the garrison surrendered
its arms. Wheeler and most of his officers were
prepared to fight to the death, for despite their
desperate plight they still held out hopes of
relief. Horne described the circumstances
under which they considered the offer:

*The situation was critical in the extreme. On
the one side, our numbers were fearfully reduced
by death and disease, gunshot, privation, and
hunger; our guns had been considerably damaged
by the enemy; and even had they not been, they
could make no adequate reply to the heavy fire
of the enemy's guns. Our ammunition was fast
coming to an end, and our food supply had run
out. With starvation staring us in the face, and
black despair in our hearts, who could blame
the wisdom of the decision that was at last
reluctantly arrived at, in favour of capitulation?*

On the following day a flag of truce
appeared over the entrenchment and the
filthy and exhausted occupants – soldiers,
women and children – were conducted down
to the Ganges at dawn on the 27th. 'Behold
us as we then appeared,' Horne recalled,

*like so many ghosts, tattered, emaciated, and
begrimed! Many a woman and child whom I had
seen enter with beautiful and smiling countenances
now looked old, haggard, desperate and imbecile.
There they stood, shoeless and stockingless, and
destitute of all the finery so dear to the heart of a
woman – objects fit to make the angels weep! The
old – battered and bruised, like ships that come
into port after being buffeted by storms – babbled
like children; others had a vacant stare in their
eyes, as if they beheld the visions of the future.
Many a little child was raving mad, and it was
pitiful to see their singular behaviour.*

The survivors rode down to the river on
elephants, escorted by rebel troops, and waded
knee-deep into the water to mount the sides
of the waiting boats, a process that took two

Massacre in the boats off Cawnpore, 27 June 1857.
Amongst all the excesses committed by the rebels, the
two massacres at Cawnpore remain the most infamous.
(Philip Haythornthwaite)

hours, for many were wounded or exhausted.
Horne and the others were unaware that
treachery was afoot. Instead of the sepoy crews
setting off with their miserable passengers,

*a signal was given from the shore and they
all leaped into the water and waded to the bank,
after having first secreted burning charcoal in the
thatch of most of the boats. Immediately a volley
of bullets assailed us, followed by a hail of shot
and grape which struck the boats. The two soldiers
seated alongside of me were wounded, and crept
into the shelter of the awning to escape being made
further targets of. In a few minutes pandemonium
reigned. Several of the boats were seen to be
wrapped in flames, and the sick and wounded were
burnt to death. Some jumped overboard and tried
to swim to the opposite shore, but were picked off
by the bullets of the sepoys. Others were drowned,
while a few jumped into the water and hid behind
their boats to escape the pitiless fire. But the guns
continued their vile work, and grape and musketry
were poured into the last-mentioned people from
the opposite bank which soon became alive with
rebels who had been placed there to intercept the
refugees to that shore. A few succeeded in pushing
their boats to the further side of the river, and were
mercilessly slaughtered.*

*The cavalry waded into the river with drawn
swords and cut down those who were still alive,
while the infantry boarded the boats ... The air
resounded with the shrieks of the women and
children and agonised prayers to God for mercy.
The water was red with blood, and the smoke
from the heavy firing of the cannon and muskets
and the fire from the burning boats lay like
dense clouds over and around us.*

Horne was one of the few survivors not
brought back into the town with the others.
Dragged to the shore by a trooper of the
3rd Bengal Cavalry, she was taken to a hut
and given Indian dress which, with her tanned
face, enabled her to appear in public without
causing notice. Some days later she underwent
a ceremony of ritual purification in which she
was forcibly converted to Islam (though she
never actually foreswore Christianity). After
several days she was taken with the rebel army
towards Allahabad, in the capacity of a guide
– for she knew the route – and was almost
rescued by British troops who routed the
mutineer column in the course of its march.
Eventually she was taken to Lucknow, even
while the Residency was under siege, and held
prisoner until the appearance of a British relief
force in the city forced her captor to flee to his
home village on the outskirts of Allahabad,
where Horne was released. She eventually
settled near Calcutta, married a railway
engineer, and lived the rest of her life in India.

The final campaigns, January–December 1858

By the end of 1857 it was clear the Mutiny could not succeed. Delhi had fallen to the British and their Indian allies, and Cawnpore and Lucknow had been relieved. Nevertheless, thousands of rebels remained in the field, no longer tied to the defence of major cities, and therefore free to manoeuvre across large distances. They no longer belonged to recognizable units, having abandoned their uniforms for civilian clothes, over which they fastened their British-issued accoutrements. Regimental distinctions had long since been effaced by the intermingling of units and the absorption of local levies and armed civilians, rendering some formations little more than guerrilla bands.

After the fall of Lucknow Campbell had hoped to rest his troops during the hot season, but Canning urged on him the necessity of recovering the largely Muslim state of Rohilkhand. The rebels, led by Khan Bahadur, were based at the capital, Bareilly, on which Campbell sent four columns to converge. On 15 April, in an ill-conceived operation, one column rashly attacked a small fort at Ruiya without properly reconnoitring its strength, and lost heavily. But thereafter operations proceeded well, and on 5 May, a few miles outside Bareilly, Khan Bahadur's forces were defeated. Exhaustion prevented the Anglo-Indians from pursuing, Khan Bahadur fled with most of his force into Oudh, and Campbell occupied Bareilly, thereby restoring British rule.

More remained for Campbell to do, for the Maulvi of Faizabad had entered Rohilkhand from Oudh with the intention of taking

Death of Brigadier-General Adrian Hope during the assault on the rebel-held fort at Ruiya, in Rohilkhand, 15 April 1858. The decision by his superior officer to launch a frontal assault without any preliminary reconnaissance cost Hope his life. (Philip Haythornthwaite)

ABOVE General Sir Hugh Rose. Though he had never served in India before, Rose adapted quickly to local conditions and in the space of only a few months dramatically demonstrated what could be achieved with a small force led by a bold and determined commander against disorganized rebels. (Philip Haythornthwaite)

no previous record of service in India. Some of the states had joined the rebellion from the start, later supported by the Rani of Jhansi, but more pressing operations elsewhere, the shortage of British troops in the area, and an especially heavy monsoon season, delayed major operations for over six months. Leading 'flying columns' totalling some 5,000–6,000 men, of whom only half were British, with Campbell moving rather more slowly, Rose conducted a masterly campaign, eventually coming to grips with the rebels and defeating them in detail. Advancing from Bombay, he first defeated troops under the Rajah of Banpur sent to relieve the fort at Rahatgarh before

Shahjahanpur. British forces obliged him to retire, but in the course of his withdrawal the Maulvi sought to bring his forces into the fort at Powain on the border with Oudh. The Rajah of Powain, however, shut the gate, and when in the act of trying to batter it down from atop an elephant, the Maulvi was shot dead. Keen to claim the 50,000-rupee reward offered by the British, the Rajah emerged from the city at a run, cut off the Maulvi's head and wrapped it in a cloth with which he appeared at the office of the magistrate at Shahjahanpur. Out rolled the head on to the dining room floor, to the delight of the magistrate, who paid over the reward. This grisly end of yet another rebel leader contributed further to the reconquest of Oudh, enabling Campbell to complete his campaign for the recovery of Rohilkhand.

In January 1858 principal responsibility for conducting final operations in central India – with Campbell playing a subsidiary role – fell to 56-year-old General Sir Hugh Rose, a man of great determination and bravery, though with

seizing the place. Then, on 3 February, Rose broke the seven-month siege of Saugor, where thousands of villagers received him rapturously as their liberator from rebel occupation.

Moving swiftly on, Rose besieged the town and fortress of Jhansi, in Bundelkhand, held by about 11,000 men, which he reached on 21 March. This place, too, had witnessed a massacre of Europeans under circumstances similar to those at Cawnpore, though on a smaller scale: 60–70 Europeans treacherously murdered after surrendering upon a promise of safe conduct to a British station. Rose duly laid siege to the city, defended by the Rani of Jhansi with over 10,000 men, only 1,500 of whom were trained sepoys, and by 30 March his artillery had made a breach in the walls. He was preparing to storm the place when news arrived of the approach of a relief force of 20,000 under Tantia Topi. Rose, unwilling to raise the siege, confronted this force with only 1,200 men (500 of whom were British), while the remainder of his army continued the siege.

Mutineers blown from the guns. At Peshawar, 40 mutineers meet their fate in the form of the old Mughal punishment for mutiny. For many Britons, the Mutiny represented a fight of the highest moral order, in defence of which, paradoxically, no mercy was shown to captured rebels. (National Army Museum)

Sir Hugh Rose, with 1,200 men (less than a third of them British) confronts 20,000 rebels under Tantia Topi outside Jhansi, 1 April 1858. After routing the mutineers and forcing them across the river Betwa, Rose prepared to assault the fortified city to oust the Rani.

His daring paid off: Tantia Topi was decisively defeated with the loss of all his guns, and the defenders of Jhansi, impressed by Rose's victory outside the city and the feint he made against the town itself, dared not issue a sortie to try to drive off the besiegers. Resting his weary men for a day, Rose then launched a full-scale attack against the city, taking the place and the fort in three days' savage fighting, with Anglo-Indian losses of 350 against the large-scale destruction of perhaps 3,000 poorly armed rebels. Aware of the massacre of the Europeans there in June, the victors handled the town's inhabitants roughly, refusing to accept the surrender of anyone bearing arms and murdering an unspecified number of civilians to boot. The Rani, disguised as a man, effected her escape to Kalpi.

The intense heat and the need to replenish his supplies required Rose to rest his troops at Jhansi for three weeks, but he was anxious to subdue the last of the rebels and capture the rebel camp at Kalpi. He first defeated the Rani and Tantia Topi at Kunch on 7 May, but the intense heat slowed his progress. The rebels stood on the brink of collapse – Tantia Topi having already gone his separate way – until a large force of cavalry under the Nawab of Banda arrived. This much-needed reinforcement, combined with encouragement given by the Rani of Jhansi and Nana Sahib's nephew, Rao Sahib, persuaded the demoralized rebels to make a final stand at Kalpi. Yet Rose's own fortunes improved with the arrival on the north bank of the Jumna of 2,000 men and eight guns sent by Campbell. Aware that the heat was causing great difficulties for Rose's troops, the rebels launched a desperate attack on 22 May which ended in their bloody repulse. During the night the rebels abandoned the city, leaving Rose to take possession of the place and its large supply of military stores on the following morning.

The fall of Kalpi marked the end of formal rebel resistance, for the mutineers were largely dispersed and had lost their last arsenal. On 1 June Rose thanked the troops and took leave of them – the same day that the combined rebel force under Tantia Topi, the Rani of Jhansi and Rao Sahib seized the city of Gwalior. There the Maharajah failed to eject them with those of his forces who had remained loyal, the remainder having already joined the mutineers some months earlier. Following a minor action at Morar the last of the Gwalior troops joined the rebels, obliging the Maharajah to flee, and leaving the great fortress at Gwalior, thought to be the strongest in India, and complete with a sizeable treasury and military stores, in rebel hands. As soon as Rose received word of this development on the 4th, he prepared to retake Gwalior, whose retention by the rebels threatened to re-ignite the rebellion. Leaving a small garrison behind at Kalpi, he left on the 6th and conducted a remarkable forced march to Gwalior, where he presumed rebel morale to be low and their power of resistance poor. His intelligence was correct, and on the 17th, in a cavalry skirmish at Kotah-ki-Serai, he decisively defeated the rebels, leaving the Rani of Jhansi, who had shown remarkable powers of leadership and bravery throughout the campaign, mortally wounded. Two days later, after 5 hours of fighting, Rose triumphantly entered the city. Tantia Topi and Rao Sahib escaped with a small contingent of their loyal followers, to spend the next several months evading pursuing Anglo-Indian troops across Rajputana, central India and Bundelkhand.

While the recapture of Gwalior and the flight of Tantia Topi and Rao Sahib signified the end of Rose's operations in central India, Oudh still remained to be subdued; that task fell to Sir Colin Campbell. After the rains ceased in October, Campbell, with 20,000 men deployed in several columns, systematically pursued the rebels for the next four months, gradually pushing them northwards towards the frontier with Nepal, destroying forts and rebel-held strongpoints in his wake. Displaying remarkable efficiency, Campbell's force achieved total success, suffering in the course of its progress fewer than a hundred casualties. Those rebels who managed to reach Nepal found themselves unwelcome to the authorities there, and many were forced back across the border, or died in the disease-infested swampland and jungles known as the Terai, or took advantage of the full pardon granted to those who discarded their weapons and peacefully returned to their homes by 1 January 1859 – provided they had had no connection with the murder of British troops or civilians.

By the end of 1858, not only had Oudh been recovered, but the remaining rebels, whose numbers probably did not exceed 25,000, had taken a precarious refuge in Nepal. Even these were flushed out when, in early 1859, at the invitation of the Nepalese authorities, an Anglo-Indian column entered the country to destroy the remaining fugitives. Some were killed, some found their way back to their homes in India, and others were taken prisoner by the Nepalese and handed over to the British, who hanged or blew from the guns any leaders of prominence.

The Mutiny, the greatest threat to British rule in India, was effectively over by the end of 1858, after a year and eight months of bitter fighting. Peace was formally proclaimed in India on 8 July 1859.

The fate of Nana Sahib, who went into hiding in Nepal, has never been definitively settled. Sources, while sometimes conflicting, suggest that he died of fever in 1860. Tantia Topi was not captured until 7 April 1859, when he was betrayed to the British and hanged 11 days later. In 1862 Rao Sahib was also betrayed, and hanged for his complicity in the Cawnpore massacres. As for Bahadur Shah, whom the mutineers had proclaimed as King of Delhi, though he was charged with rebellion and complicity in the murder of Europeans, his life was spared. His actual cooperation with the rebels was open to question, for he appeared to have been a victim of circumstances: once Delhi had been occupied his support for the rebel cause could not be refused. With these mitigating circumstances in mind, and with a desire not to create a martyr, British authorities exiled the last heir to the Mughal Empire to Rangoon, where he died in 1862.

The effects of the Mutiny on the Raj

While the Mutiny failed to eliminate the westernizing influence of British rule, British victory did not give *carte blanche* to those who would continue the process of transforming Indian society on the British model. Within two years of the conflict rule was indeed reasserted across the sub-continent, yet relations between the belligerents could not be re-established on entirely the same basis of trust. The anger and animosity to which the fighting and, above all, the atrocities had given rise gradually eased, but the conflict understandably exacerbated the social and cultural differences which had always existed between the two societies, and the contempt in which some Britons held Indians intensified. The practice by which British communities were living in increasing physical isolation from Indians grew more widespread, and contact, except as business required it, grew less frequent. The horrific nature of the fighting heightened the British

Government House, Calcutta, home of Lord and Lady Canning. Outwardly impressive, this classical structure was in fact oppressively hot unless the windows were tightly closed and the Venetian blinds lowered. Water-closets were entirely absent, while massive cockroaches and red ants infested the place, lizards and red ants climbed the walls and furniture, and bats flew through the bedrooms.

sense of cultural and racial superiority, though it did not always manifest itself in obvious displays of contempt, particularly where Indians of high social rank were concerned. Still, British officials expected and received a reasonable degree of deference from the indigenous population, and instances of arrogance were not uncommon amongst colonists and administrators who saw themselves as the purveyors of justice, law, true faith, enlightened thought, and superior science and technology.

After the Mutiny instances of racial abuse increased, albeit gradually, and the more benevolent attitudes best associated with the 18th century largely gave way to civility at best and disdain at worst. In the wake of the Mutiny the rapid influx of British settlers – encouraged to remain in India by the British government as a possible means of rendering future rebellion less likely – lent strength to such attitudes, for this new generation had no prior connection with the sub-continent, and thus it possessed no natural affinity for the place and its people. Indeed, India increasingly became attractive not to those possessing a reforming spirit or a desire to administer the colony for its own benefit, but rather to businessmen keen to exploit

View of Salsoor, in the Deccan, the heartland of the Marathas, with its capital at Hyderabad. Despite the general threat of a rising throughout this region, few mutinies occurred and most were foiled from the outset.

the large profits to be derived from tea and coffee plantations and cheap uncultivated land in the hills which new legislation made available them.

It was natural enough that this new wave of Britons, knowing nothing of Indian culture and tradition and heavily influenced by the stories of the atrocities during the Mutiny should arrive with strong prejudices against the Indian population. The notion that British rule symbolized a sort of stewardship over a people who might eventually rule themselves was utter nonsense to most such newcomers, who preferred the interpretation that, as God had granted Britain guardianship over a vast, sprawling empire on the basis of her racial and cultural superiority, settlers ought to be free to exploit the population as they saw fit. Prior to the Mutiny the notion of racial superiority had of course always existed, yet previous generations of administrators had regarded themselves as fulfilling a higher

mission, whether it was to convert Indians to Christianity or to introduce what they regarded as the benefits of their civilization. These notions were largely absent from the minds of those who ventured to India in the second half of the 19th century.

As religion had played a major role in the origins of the Mutiny, it was natural that in the wake of the conflict the British should reassess the role evangelism ought thereafter to play in India. It was clear to nearly everyone that attempts to Christianize the sub-continent – never part of official policy and largely the work of missionary societies – had ended disastrously. Clearly, those who before the Mutiny had worked and prayed for conversion on a large scale had utterly failed to predict the backlash, and for many Christians their ardour received a severe check in light of the bitter lessons learned. Neither Hinduism nor Islam had stood aside in favour of Christianity, and those religious practices which Britons regarded as distasteful, even shocking, superstition and ignorance – at least in the religious realm – would for the most part be permitted to carry on unmolested.

If India was ever to be Christianized and to join the ranks of what mid-Victorians regarded as the civilized nations of the world, it was clearly not going to happen in the short term. With their illusions dispelled, most Britons grew to accept, if perhaps grudgingly, Hinduism and Islam as fixtures of Indian life, with the work of the preceding generation of missionaries acknowledged to have secured only a few converts. The overriding lesson of the Mutiny was indeed a stark one: any serious attempt, real or perceived, to spread the Christian faith in India constituted an almost certainly futile, if not downright provocative, enterprise.

Naturally, a few diehards remained. Indeed, the most passionate evangelicals amongst these turned the lesson of the Mutiny on its head: for them the revolt was divine punishment for the British having led dissolute lives in India and for having failed to proselytize *more* fervently. Missionary work should be redoubled – not reigned in. No less than David Livingstone himself, who had sought to bring Christianity to 'darkest' Africa, delivered a rousing message on the subject to the Senate House at Cambridge University:

I consider we made a great mistake when we carried commerce into India, in being ashamed of our Christianity… Those two pioneers of civilization – Christianity and commerce – should ever be inseparable; and Englishmen should be warned by the fruits of neglecting that principle as exemplified in the management of Indian affairs.

At about the same time, a missionary in Benares went almost so far as to welcome the bloodshed that had recently engulfed the sub-continent when he expressed his conviction that

Instead of giving way to despondency, well does it become us to brace ourselves anew for our Master's work, in the full assurance that our labour will not be in vain. Satan will again be defeated. He doubtless intended, by this rebellion, to drive the Gospel from India; but he has only prepared the way, as often before in the history of the Church, for its wider diffusion.

In the event, such notions, intended by their advocates to take on practical forms – with Bible classes to be taught all government schools and prisons, and the possibility of non-observance of Hindu and Islamic holidays – found no support from British government authorities in Calcutta, where the overwhelming body of opinion believed that a policy of strict religious neutrality was needed more than ever.

The realization that Christianity could not be expected to make a substantial appearance in India went hand in hand with an acceptance that British rule might not succeed in introducing other aspects of Western civilisation; that is to say, with no fundamental change to morals, and a failure to eradicate superstitions and customs regarded as backward, such as polygamy, child marriage and perhaps even the caste system itself. Whereas before Indians might be rendered Britons in terms of attitude, opinions, morals and education, even progressive-minded Britons – while never doubting the moral imperative of their aims – began to question whether attempting fundamentally to transform Indian society was in fact a realistic prospect. While the British may in their eyes have possessed a special mandate to raise the moral consciousness of the Indian people through education and good example, after the Mutiny many administrators and colonists came to view Indians as irredeemably lost, at least in the short term, merely to be ruled rather than improved.

Thus, perhaps the greatest consequences of the Mutiny were two-fold: a general halt in the hitherto vigorous efforts of missionaries to convert Indians on a large scale; and a slowing of the process by which administrators of the Raj sought to 'civilise' the country with Britain as its model. Only a small minority of people supported the idea of preparing Indians for self-government through education, much less employing them in large numbers in the administration of their own country. Indians were admitted to junior positions in the civil service, but this process was highly regulated, and a deliberate policy of exclusion from the higher ranks of administration could be justified on the grounds that only a handful of Indians were fit for the task.

Having said this, in light of the catastrophe of recent years, Lord Canning appreciated that to exclude Indians altogether from higher decisions of government would be a grave mistake, and admitted onto the Legislative Council, which advised the government in Calcutta, a small number of Indian representatives. This posed no threat to British rule, for supreme control of executive affairs would remain with the government, and in any event the Governor-General could assume emergency powers for six months if circumstances required it. Canning therefore nominated three prominent aristocratic Indians to the Council, on the basis that they had provided useful assistance to his government during the Mutiny. In short, despite the presence of a rising class of Indians educated in the British manner, no such men were invited to the higher echelons of imperial administration with the exception already identified. Other reforms included the Indian Councils Act of 1861, which established local legislative bodies, to include at least one Indian representative each, in Madras, Bombay and Bengal. Thus, British authorities exercised a modicum of foresight in opening up the civil service to a limited number of Indians themselves.

The Mutiny also revealed the need to reform the system of law courts in India, as well as of the law itself. The judicial system, which had remained largely unchanged since 1773, contained two separate strands. The first was managed by East India Company officials who administered Hindu, Muslim, and English law. The second consisted of three Supreme Courts operated separately – one each at Calcutta, Bombay, and Madras, where Crown officials, including many judges sent out from Britain, administered English law to both Indians and British subjects living within the three presidencies. As the two systems were incompatible and blurred the boundaries of authority between them, the India High Courts Act of 1861 amalgamated the two, creating three High Courts, with a fourth established at Allahabad in 1866 with

similar institutions – all exercising jurisdiction over civil and criminal courts within the territories of their respective presidencies – created in the Punjab, Sind and central India. Though the great majority of High Court judges were crown-appointed, they were to be drawn from several categories in equal numbers: members of the Indian Civil Service (all of whom were British); barristers sent out from Britain; and lawyers who had practiced in India. The broad definition of this last category was deliberate, for it enabled Indians themselves to play a small role in the legal system. Accordingly, shortly after the Mutiny, Canning appointed an Indian judge to the Calcutta High Court, partly as a means of demonstrating that his government was sincere in its desire to expand Indians' participation in their own affairs – albeit on an extremely limited scale.

British officials also undertook the reform of Indian law itself. Muslim criminal law, which had undergone alteration over time, nevertheless remained in force, with its procedure hamstrung by an antiquated system of civil and criminal courts subject to complex regulations. To tackle these problems, a law commission established in London in 1853 and seeking to build on proposals for fundamental reform drawn up twenty-five years earlier, compiled the historic *Codes of Civil and of Criminal Procedure* in the years immediately preceding the Mutiny. These were adopted between 1859 and 1861 and replaced the existing body of Muslim law, providing a standard legal framework that applied across the entire sub-continent.

Thus, in the short-term, the British in India gleaned a few clear lessons from the Mutiny: the sub-continent could no longer be regarded as fruitful ground for religious conversion, nor could a positive reception to British ideas on morality, opinion, culture and politics be taken for granted. Yet while it was widely understood that concessions ought to, and would be, made to Indians, there was no sense that self-rule – in which direction 'white' colonies like Canada and Australia were already moving – was anything but a very distant prospect indeed.

Why the Mutiny failed; British post-war reforms

Why the Mutiny failed

On the face of it, the revolt ought to have succeeded. For generations most officers in the forces of the East India Company had taken the loyalty of the sepoy troops for granted, and when the dam finally did burst, British authorities found themselves caught entirely off guard and, at least at the outset, forced to operate under very disadvantageous circumstances. In the longer term, however, the mutineers enjoyed only limited advantages, and the reasons for their failure may be attributed to several factors.

First, the Mutiny failed to attract widespread support from Indian civilians. Indeed, the revolt was restricted to various disaffected Indian rulers and parts of the Bengal Army. The vast majority of civilians living in the countryside remained neutral or apathetic, or provided some sympathy but little real support to the mutineers. Only in Oudh was there evidence of genuine patriotic support and a degree of loyalty towards the deposed nawab. Only there did British forces regularly consider themselves in hostile territory. While rebellion took root in parts of other regions, such as in the North-West Provinces and Bundelkhand, and in the south-eastern portion of the Punjab, these areas contained dispossessed landowners and minor chiefs who hoped to regain their power and territory, not hostile populations eager to throw off British rule. The comparatively few princes and rulers who supported the Mutiny comprised the last vestiges of a declining feudal order

Execution of mutineers at Peshawar. For many Britons, the Mutiny represented a fight of the highest moral order, not least because the rebels' massacre of European women and children was seen as the most abominable of all crimes. (Philip Haythornthwaite)

whose days under British rule were clearly
numbered. Thus it may be said that most of
those who supported the revolt were looking
to the defence of the old order, rather than
seeking a progressive new India.

Practically everywhere else across the
sub-continent, however, other Indians –
including nearly all of the major ruling
chiefs – actually assisted British civil and
military authorities in their efforts to
suppress rebellion, while some ordinary
Indians risked their own lives to hide

The 'Well of the Innocents', Cawnpore. A protective
white marble angel stands guard over the resting place
of the victims of the second massacre. Soon after Indian
independence the statue and screen were removed to
the grounds of All Saints' Church, beside the site of
Wheeler's entrenchment. Today the well is covered
by an unmarked concrete slab. (British Empire and
Commonwealth Museum)

fugitives from the rebels. The leaders
of the Punjab, in particular, despite their
recent conflict with the British, remained
unswervingly loyal to their erstwhile

enemies during the crisis years of 1857–58, as did the Maharajah of Sindhia and the Nizam of Hyderabad.

The absence of any coherent plan also doomed the Mutiny to failure. Apart from the fact that the revolt did not take hold throughout India generally – which would almost certainly have ended the Raj at a stroke – it is important to note that the rising was neither planned nor stimulated by any patriotic motive. While the ostensible cause of the revolt was the defence of religion, the mutineers soon ceased to fight primarily with this in view. In fact, no clear purpose arose, and no unifying principle, around which the movement could coalesce, emerged.

Evidence of wide-scale looting of fellow Indians on the part of the mutineers reveals that many simply took advantage of the absence of the forces of law and order to profit for themselves wherever and whenever they could. The King of Delhi did not prove the charismatic leader of a clearly defined political cause: his aim amounted to little more than the eradication of British rule without the benefit of any plan for its

replacement by an indigenous ruling structure. Indeed, although rebel leaders gradually came to the fore, they generally failed to coordinate their efforts in the field, and appear to have desired only regional political power for themselves.

In addition to a lack of direction and purpose, the rebels were unable to produce much in the way of competent military commanders or to implement a coordinated strategy. While they enjoyed an overwhelming advantage in sheer numbers, they failed to destroy British forces in the north in the early stages of the Mutiny; instead, most of the rebels concentrated in a static defence of Delhi. Worse still, they suffered from weaknesses at both the strategic and tactical levels. By rebelling, the mutineers in effect decapitated their command structure and, in the absence of any immediately available natural

Lord Canning visiting the Punjab, March 1860. Although dubbed 'Clemency Canning' by his critics for the leniency he extended to former rebels, the Viceroy laid the groundwork for decades of peaceful rule and tolerance across the whole sub-continent. (British Library)

leadership, instead looked for ad hoc leaders to rise to the fore. True, they were well trained, well armed, acclimatized, strongly motivated, fighting on home ground, and on average outnumbered their opponents by more than seven to one; yet their numerical superiority was compromised by poor leadership at battalion level and above, as well by the absence of any proper command structure with which to coordinate operations either between elements of the same force, or with other rebel formations. Even where overwhelming numbers ought to have translated into success – as at the numerous assaults conducted during the sieges of Delhi, Cawnpore and Lucknow – they consistently failed to take their objectives. Such consistent tactical failures must be attributed to poor unit cohesion, as well as poor leadership. As the primary loyalty of the sepoy was to his regiment, once these bonds were severed regimental discipline became weakened – or dissolved altogether – and soldiers became individuals in a vast armed mob, the basis of whose unit integrity rested on common survival and the acquisition of loot.

The Mutiny cannot be reduced to a simplistic contest between Briton and Indian. Considerable credit for the maintenance of British control in some regions, and the re-assertion of imperial rule in others, must unquestionably be given to the Indian troops who fought on the British side. Indeed, the majority of soldiers serving the Raj were in fact themselves Indians: approximately half the troops on the Ridge at Delhi were Indians, and 80 per cent of the soldiers killed on the British side during the siege were recorded as 'native'. Seven hundred of the defenders of the Residency at Lucknow were loyal Indians, as were thousands of those who came to its relief. Without the crucial contribution made to the British cause by loyal Indian forces, who performed countless acts of bravery and displayed steadfastness throughout the conflict, colonial rule in India might very well have come to an end.

British post-war reforms

The Mutiny came as such a shock to the British government that it was compelled to adopt a new method for the governance of India. As the East India Company could no longer be relied upon to administer the sub-continent on behalf of the Crown, in 1858 Parliament voted the Act for the Better Government of India, which on 2 August formally transferred control from the East India Company to the Crown. Thereafter India would be directly governed by Britain through the Secretary of State for India, to whom the Viceroy (the office replacing that of Governor-General) would be accountable. On 1 November Canning, who continued at his post in Calcutta, issued a proclamation, read in cities across India, announcing these reforms, offered an amnesty to all rebels who had not themselves murdered British subjects, or who were not leaders of the revolt, and, by publicizing the Queen's renunciation of 'the right and the desire to impose Our convictions on any of Our subjects,' recognized the legitimacy of Indian grievances against the spread of Christianity. In the wake of the Mutiny successive viceroys tolerated, rather than encouraged, missionary societies in India, and took greater heed of Indian religious sensitivities.

Some of the most wide-ranging reforms naturally affected the armed forces in India. With the extinction of the Company came the disbandment of its forces and the transfer of most of its British officers and men into the Queen's forces. Batteries composed entirely of British soldiers were amalgamated into the Royal Artillery, while nine infantry units with British personnel became regiments of the line or light infantry in the British Army. In 1858, cavalry units meant exclusively for service in India and adjacent areas were recruited in Britain, with cadres from mounted units formerly under Company control. Three years later these units were disbanded, with some of

End of the Raj: the lowering of the British flag from atop the ruins of the Residency at Lucknow, 15 August 1947. A Union flag flew perpetually on this spot for nearly 90 years – from the retaking of the Residency in March 1858 until the day India received its independence. (Illustrated London News)

their personnel renewing their period of service as three newly created regiments of Light Dragoons in the British Army. British personnel of the former Indian engineer corps were transferred to the Royal Engineers.

The three presidencies – Bengal, Madras and Bombay – were not eradicated in the post-war reforms, and thus their respective armies remained in existence, albeit totally reconstituted, reorganized and collectively known as the Indian Army. As the Bengal Army, largely destroyed during the Mutiny, had supplied the bulk of the rebel forces, it naturally became subject to the most sweeping reforms of any of the former Company's armies. During the revolt every cavalry regiment of the Bengal Army had rebelled, though a number of mounted irregular units had been raised for service with British forces. In 1861 these were formed into 19 regular cavalry regiments, and 12 of the Bengal Native Infantry regiments which still existed

at the end of the Mutiny were re-numbered and retained in service; three regiments were disbanded, and the remainder, up to number 44, were created from irregular units which had existed before the rebellion or been raised during it, and also by adding regiments recruited in the Punjab, Gwalior and Assam. Four regiments were later redesignated as Gurkhas and removed from the Bengal, to the British Army.

The Madras Army, with the exception of a few units, remained utterly loyal to British authority, and therefore underwent only minor changes after 1858, with one light cavalry regiment being disbanded during the Mutiny on account of its refusal to serve in Bengal, followed by three others at the end of 1860. Only two battalions of the Bombay Army served the rebels during the Mutiny, but these were made good by the addition of infantry from other units. The various irregular foot and mounted units raised during the fighting were gradually phased out between 1861 and 1865. By the time the reorganization of the armed forces in India had been completed, the proportion of British to Indian troops was far greater than ever before: 65,000 of the former and 140,000 of the latter, a much greater proportion of whom were drawn from the so-called 'martial races' of the north, in preference to recruits from the traditional recruiting grounds of central and southern India. Troops from the north, such as the Sikhs drawn from the Punjab, had shown loyalty and tenacity – ideal attributes of the fighting man – and thus became the mainstay of the Indian Army.

It is a testament to the remarkable transformation in Anglo-Indian relations that, in the nearly 90 years between the end of the Mutiny and the creation of the independent dominions of India and Pakistan in 1947, the Indian Army fought loyally for the British Empire in numerous conflicts, above all in the First and Second World Wars, in the latter of which 2 million Indians served.

Further reading

Only scant historical documentation exists from the mutineers' perspective, obliging the reader to rely almost exclusively on British material for any understanding of the conflict. Fortunately, this is available in abundance.

Primary sources

Adye, Sir John Miller, *Recollections of a Military Life*, New York: Macmillan and Co., 1895.

Alexander, William Gordon, *Recollections of a Highland Subaltern, During the Campaigns of the 93rd Highlanders in India Under Colin Campbell*, London: Edward Arnold, 1898.

Anson, O.H.S.G., *With H.M. 9th Lancers During the Indian Mutiny: The Letters of Brevet-Major O.H.S.G. Anson*, Uckfield, East Sussex: Naval and Military Press.

Bonham, John, *Oude in 1857: Some Memories of the Indian Mutiny*, London: Williams & Norgate, 1928.

Bourchier, George, *Eight months' Campaign against the Bengal Sepoy Army during the Mutiny of 1857*, Uckfield, East Sussex: Naval & Military Press, 2004 (reprint of 1858 edition).

Broehl, Wayne G., *Crisis of the Raj: The Revolt of 1857 through a British Lieutenant's Eyes*, Hanover, NH: University Press of New England, 1986.

Germon, Maria, *Journal of the Siege of Lucknow: An Episode of the Indian Mutiny*, London: Constable, 1958.

Gowing, Timothy, *A Soldier's Experience, or, a Voice from the Ranks*, Nottingham: T. Forman, 1899.

Grant, Sir James Hope, *Incidents in the Sepoy War, 1857–58, Compiled from the Private Journals of General Sir Hope Grant*, London: W. Blackwood, 1873.

Gray, Robert, *Reminiscences of India and North Queensland, 1857–1912*, London: Constable and Co., 1913.

Griffiths, Charles, *A Narrative of the Siege of Delhi with an Account of the Mutiny at Ferozepore in 1857*, London: John Murray, 1910.

Harris, Georgina, *A Lady's Diary of the Siege of Lucknow*, London, 1858.

Jones, Oliver, *Recollections of a Winter Campaign in India, 1857–58*, Uckfield, East Sussex: Naval & Military Press, 2002 (reprint of 1859 edition).

Keene, H.G., *Fifty-Seven: Some Account of the Administration in Indian Districts During the Revolt of the Bengal Army*, London: W.H. Allen, 1883.

Knight, Ian, *Queen Victoria's Enemies (3)*, Oxford: Osprey Publishing, 1990.

Lang, Arthur (edited by David Blomfield), *Lahore to Lucknow: The Indian Mutiny Journal of Arthur Moffat Lang*, London: Leo Cooper, 1992.

Lee, J., *The Indian Mutiny; Events at Cawnpore*, Cawnpore: Medical Hall Press, 1886.

Mackenzie, Alfred, *Mutiny Memoirs: Being Personal Reminiscences of the Great Sepoy Revolt of 1857*, Allahabad: Pioneer Press, 1891.

Maude, Edwin, *Oriental Campaigns and European Furloughs: The Autobiography of a Veteran of the Indian Mutiny*, London: T.F. Unwin, 1908.

Muter, Elizabeth, *My Recollections of the Sepoy Revolt (1857–58)*, London: John Long, 1911

Ouvry, M.H., *A Lady's Diary Before and During the Indian Mutiny*, Lymington: C.T. King, 1892.

Roberts, Lord Frederick Sleigh, *Forty-One Years in India: from Subaltern to Commander-in-chief*, 2 vols, London: Macmillan, 1905.

—————————, *Letters Written During the Indian Mutiny*, London: Macmillan & Co., 1924.

Russell, William Howard, *My Indian Mutiny Diary*, London: Cassell, 1957.

Seton, Rosemary E., *The Indian Mutiny, 1857–58: A Guide to Source Material in the India Office Library and Records*, London: British Library, 1986.

Stewart, Charles, *Through Persia in Disguise; With Reminiscences of the Indian Mutiny*, London: G. Routledge and Sons, 1911.

Strathnairn, Hugh Henry Rose, Baron (edited by Brian Robson), *Sir Hugh Rose and the Central India Campaign, 1858*, Stroud, Glos: Sutton Publishing for the Army Records Society, 2000.

Thornhill, Mark, *The Personal Adventures and Experiences of a Magistrate During the Rise, Progress, and Suppression of the Indian Mutiny*, London: J. Murray, 1884.

Tisdall, Evelyn, *Mrs. Duberly's Campaigns: An Englishwoman's Experiences in the Crimean War and the Indian Mutiny*, London: Jarrolds, 1963.

Walker, Thomas Nicolls, *Through the Mutiny: Reminiscences of Thirty Years' Active Service and Sport in India, 1854–83*, London: Gibbings & Co., 1907.

Wilberforce, Reginald Garton, *An Unrecorded Chapter of the Indian Mutiny: Being the Personal Reminiscences of Reginald G. Wilberforce, late 52nd Light Infantry, Compiled from a Diary and Letters Written on the Spot*, London: J. Murray, 1895.

Wilson, Thomas, *The Defence of Lucknow: A Diary, Recording the Daily Events During the Siege of the European Residency, from 31st May to 25th September, 1857*, London: Smith, Elder, 1858.

Young, Keith (edited by General Sir Henry Wylie Norman and Mrs Keith Young), *Delhi 1857: The Siege, Assault and Capture as given in the Diary and Correspondence of the late Colonel Keith Young, C.B., Judge-Advocate General, Bengal*, Uckfield, East Sussex: Naval and Military Press, 2004.

Secondary sources

Ahmed Khan, Sayed, *The Causes of the Indian Revolt*, Karachi: Oxford University Press, 2000.

Bayly, C. A., ed., *The Peasant Armed: The Indian Revolt of 1857*, Oxford: Clarendon Press, 1986.

_____, *Indian Society and the Making of the British Empire*, Cambridge: Cambridge University Press, 1988.

Collier, Richard, *The Great Indian Mutiny: A Dramatic Account of the Sepoy Rebellion*, New York: Dutton, 1964.

Dalrymple, William, *The Last Mughal: The Fall of a Dynasty, Delhi 1857*, London: Bloomsbury, 2006.

_____, *White Mughals: Love and Betrayal in Eighteenth Century India*, London: HarperPerennial, 2003.

Dangerfield, George, *Bengal Mutiny: The Story of the Sepoy Rebellion*, New York: Harcourt, Brace and Company, 1933.

David, Saul, *The Indian Mutiny: 1857*, London: Viking, 2002.

De Rhe Philipe, George and Miles Irving, *Soldiers of the Raj*, 3 vols, Uckfield, East Sussex: Naval and Military Press, 2002.

Edwardes, Michael, *Battles of the Indian Mutiny*, London: Batsford, 1963.

_____, *Red Year: The Indian Rebellion of 1857*, London: Hamilton, 1973.

Embree, Ainslie, *1857 in India: Mutiny or War of Independence?*, Boston: Heath, 1963.

Featherstone, Donald, *Victorian Colonial Warfare: India*, London: Blandford, 1993.

Fortescue, Sir J.W., *A History of the British Army*, 20 vols. (vol. xiii), reprint, Uckfield, East Sussex: Naval and Military Press, 2002.

Gilmour, David, *The Ruling Caste: Imperial Lives in the Victorian Raj*, London: John Murray, 2005.

Haythornthwaite, Philip J, *The Colonial Wars Source Book*, London: Arms and Armour Press, 1995.

Harris, John, *The Indian Mutiny*, London: Hart-Davis MacGibbon, 1973.

Heathcote, T. A., *The Indian Army: The Garrison of British Imperial India, 1822–1922*, Newton Abbott, Devon: David & Charles, 1974.

Hibbert, Christopher, *The Great Mutiny: India, 1857*, London: Penguin, 1980.

Holmes, Richard, *Sahib: The British Soldier in India, 1750–1914*, London: HarperCollins, 2005.

Hoppen, K. Theodore, *The Mid-Victorian Generation, 1846–1886*, Oxford: Clarendon Press, 1998.

James, Lawrence, *Raj: The Making and Unmaking of British India*, London: Abacus, 1998.

_____, *The Rise and Fall of the British Empire*, London: Abacus, 1995.

Judd, Denis, *The Lion and the Tiger: The Rise and Fall of the British Raj, 1600–1947*, Oxford: Oxford University Press, 2004.

Keay, John, *The Honourable Company: A History of the English East India Company*, London: HarperCollins, 1993.

Kingsley, D. A., *They Fight like Devils: Stories from Lucknow During the Great Indian Mutiny, 1857–58*, New York: Sarpedon, 2001.

Knight, Ian, *Go to your God like a Soldier: The British Soldier Fighting for Empire, 1837–1902*, London: Greenhill Books, 1996.

Leasor, James, *The Red Fort*, London: Collier Books, 1982.

Llewellyn, Alexander, *The Siege of Delhi*, London: Macdonald and James, 1977.

Lowe, Thomas, *Operations of the British Army in Central India during the Rebellion of 1857 and 1858*, Uckfield, East Sussex: Naval and Military Press, 2002 (reprint of 1860 edition).

Kaye, Sir J. and G. B. Malleson, *Kaye and Malleson's History of the Indian Mutiny of 1857–58*, 6 vols, Uckfield, East Sussex: Naval and Military Press, 2003 (reprint of 1897 edition).

Metcalf, T. R., *The Aftermath of Revolt: India, 1857–1870*, Princeton: Princeton University Press, 1965.

Morris, Jan, *Heaven's Command: An Imperial Progress*, London: Faber and Faber.

Mukherjee, Rudrangshu, *Awadh in Revolt, 1857–1858: A Study of Popular Resistance*, Delhi: Oxford University Press, 1984.

Palmer, J. A. B., *The Mutiny Outbreak at Meerut in 1857*, Cambridge: Cambridge University Press, 1966.

Pemble, John, *The Raj, the Indian Mutiny and the Kingdom of Oudh, 1801–1859*, Hassocks: Harvester Press, 1977.

Perrett, Bryan, *At all Costs! Stories of Impossible Victories*, London: Arms and Armour Press, 1994.

_____, *Impossible Victories: Ten Unlikely Battlefield Successes*, London: Arms and Armour Press, 1998.

Porter, Andrew, ed., *The Oxford History of the British Empire: The Nineteenth Century*, Oxford: Oxford University Press, 1999.

Robinson, Jane, *Angels of Albion: Women of the Indian Mutiny*, London: Viking, 1996.

Roy, Tapti, *The Politics of a Popular Uprising: Bundelkhand in 1857*, New York: Oxford University Press, 1994.

Smyth, John George, Sir, *The Rebellious Rani*, London: Muller, 1966.

Spear, T. G. P., *The Oxford History of Modern India, 1740–1947*, New York: Oxford University Press, 1978.

Taylor, P. J. O. (ed.), *A Companion to the Indian Mutiny of 1857*, New York: Oxford University Press, 1996.

_____, *What Really Happened During the Mutiny: A Day-by-day Account of the Major Events of 1857–1859 in India*, New York: Oxford University Press, 1997.

Thompson, Edward, *The Other Side of the Medal*, Westport, CT: Greenwood Press, 1974.

Venning, Annabel, *Following the Drum: The Lives of Army Wives and Daughters*, London: Headline Book Publishing, 2005.

Ward, Andrew, *Our Bones are Scattered: the Cawnpore Massacre and the Indian Mutiny of 1857*, New York: Henry Holt and Co., 1996.

Watson, Bruce, *The Great Indian Mutiny: Colin Campbell and the Campaign at Lucknow*, New York: Praeger, 1991.

Index